JN084361

NHK WORLD JAPAN

NHK
Tatsuroh Yamazaki
Stella M.Yamazaki
NEWSLINE 6

KINSEIDO

Kinseido Publishing Co., Ltd.

3-21 Kanda Jimbo-cho, Chiyoda-ku,
Tokyo 101-0051, Japan

First published 2023 by Kinseido Publishing Co., Ltd.

Video materials NHK (Japan Broadcasting Corporation)

Authors and publisher are grateful to NHK Global Media
Services, Inc. and all the interviewees who appeared on
the news.

はじめに

　NHK NEWSLINE のテキストシリーズが刊行されてから、本書で 6 冊目を迎えることができた。これも皆さま方のご支援によるもので心より感謝申し上げる。

　日本の英語教育が国際的にあまり評価されていないとは言え、少しずつ伸びているのは確かである。文科省によれば、英語能力試験の結果は毎年右肩上がりで、令和 3 年の高校生の CEFR A2（英検準 2 級レベル）相当（以上）の割合は 46.1%（10 年前は 30.4%）である。また高校の英語教師も、令和 3 年で CEFR B2（英検準 1 級レベル）相当（以上）の割合は 74.9%（8 年前は 52.7%）となっている。しかし、国際的信頼を得るためには、グローバルなコミュニケーションの手段としての英語に更に拍車をかけなければならない。

　日本ではオミクロン株変異種への感染拡大により、都市部の大学などでは対面授業が完全復活を果たしていない。しかし外出自粛が推奨される中、それを逆手にとって学生の皆さんは自宅でじっくり実力を養う好機ととらえることもできる。オンラインの英会話レッスンは、安全にしてかつ効果が期待できる。それと並行して、会話の前提となるリスニング能力を伸ばす本書のような教材も積極的に活用できる。

　会話は音声のインプットとアウトプットの合わせ技だが、外国語は徹底的に聞いて模倣するという姿勢が常に必要である。従って伝統的な反復練習や文型練習は、語学学習者にとって必修である。目で追うだけではなく何回か反復して「音読」しておこう。音読しておけば記憶に定着しやすく、会話でもとっさの時に出てくるという利点がある。学習者にとって外国語の会話は（運動競技と同様に）スキルであり、練習によって積み上げた「記憶」が頼りなのである。

　本書はリスニングを中心課題に据えたニュースの視聴覚教材である。ニュースは NHK 海外向け放送の *NEWSLINE* から採択し、適切な長さに編集した。この番組は現代日本の主な出来事や経済、文化、科学の最近の動向などを簡潔にまとめており好評を博している。

　語学は授業中の学習だけではじゅうぶんではない。現在、ニュース映像がオンラインで視聴可能となった。自宅で納得するまで繰り返し見てほしい。その際、まず完成したスクリプト（News Story の穴埋め問題終了後）を見ながら音声と意味の対応を頭に入れ、その後は文字を見ないで聞くという作業が必要である。この繰り返しが何回かあれば、文字なしで映像音声の理解ができるという快感が味わえるようになる。

　末筆ながら、本書の作成に関して金星堂編集部をはじめ関係スタッフの方々に大変お世話になった。更に出版にあたって NHK、株式会社 NHK グローバルメディアサービスの皆様にも映像提供などで御協力をいただいた。ここに厚くお礼を申し上げる。

2023 年 1 月　　　　　　　　　　　　　　編著者：山﨑達朗／ Stella M. Yamazaki

本書の構成とねらい

　本書は全部で 15 単元 (units) からなり、各単元とも、①日本語のイントロダクション、② Words & Phrases、③ Before You Watch、④ Watch the News、⑤ Understand the News、⑥ Listen to the News Story、⑦ Review the Key Expressions、⑧ Discussion Questions という構成になっている。このうち①と②は説明で、③〜⑧が練習問題である。

① 日本語のイントロダクション

この短い日本語の説明（約 140 語）は、ニュースの要点を把握することを目的としている。外国語のリスニングには、何がどのように飛び出してくるかわからないという緊張と不安が常に伴うので、このように限られた背景知識（background knowledge）でも、予め準備があると安心感が出るものである。

② Words & Phrases

比較的難しいか、カギになる語彙や熟語などを学習する。ここで意味的、文法的知識をつけておけば、ニュースを聞いた場合に戸惑いは少なくなる。必要に応じて簡単な例文も入れてある。

③ Before You Watch

ニュース映像を見る前に、その予備知識を獲得したり話題を膨らませたりする意味で単元ごとに違った課題が用意してある。内容的には、日常会話表現の学習であったり、社会・文化に特有な語彙を英語でどう言うかといった課題であったりする。方法としても活動に興味が持てるように、ややゲーム的な要素も入れるようにしてある。英語の語彙を縦横に並んだアルファベット表から見つけ出すタスクや、クロスワードの活用もその例である。

④ Watch the News — 1st Viewing

ここで初めてクラスで映像を見るわけだが、課題はニュース内容の大きな流れや要点の理解が主となる基本的把握である。設問が 3 つあり、各問とも内容に合っていれば T（= True）、合っていなければ F（= False）を選択し、問題文の真偽を判断する。外国語のリスニングはしぜんに耳から入ってくるということがないので、集中して聞く必要がある。必要に応じて随時、視聴の回数を増やしたり、問題と関連する箇所を教師が集中的に見せたりするということが過去の経験から有効である。

⑤ Understand the News — 2nd Viewing

同じニュース映像をもう一度見るが、内容についてのやや詳細な質問となっている。次の2種類の下位区分がある。ここも必要に応じ、複数回のリスニングを考慮してほしい。

1 最初の視聴と比べて今度は選択肢が3つになっており、内容もより詳細にわたる設問が用意してある。各問、左端の3枚の写真は、参考にはなるが、問題を解く上でリスニングのキーとなる部分の映像とは限らないので注意してほしい。

2 単元によって、何種類か様々な形式の設問が用意してある。いずれもニュース内容の確認を目的としている。例えばニュースのまとめとなる「概要」や「入手情報の順序づけ」、要点となる数字の記入などである。さらに、設問によっては、ややゲーム的な要素を考慮し、アルファベットの並べ替え（unscrambling）を入れている。

⑥ Listen to the News Story

これはニュース映像に対応するスクリプトであるが、完全なものにするには「穴埋め問題」を解く必要がある。問題は合計7問で、各問題に6～7か所の空所がある。解答するには，スタジオでややゆっくり読まれた音声CDをクラスで（各2回繰り返し）聞きながら書き取り作業（dictation）をする。スクリプトのそれぞれの問題には、右端におおよその日本語訳（数字以外）が付けてあるのでヒントになる。書き取りが完成すればニュース映像の全文が目で確かめられるが、スクリプトは映像を見る前に読むことはせず、まず何回か視聴して上記④と⑤の設問に解答した後に、この穴埋めに挑戦してほしい。

⑦ Review the Key Expressions

ここでは、映像で出てきた単語や熟語などのうち応用性のある表現に習熟することがねらいである。そのような重要表現の意味や用法を確実にするとともに、英作文があまり負担なく身につくように単語を与える「整序問題」形式（4問）を採用した。ただし選択肢の中に錯乱肢（distractors）を1語入れ、適度に難しくしてある。文例は当該単元の話題とは関係なく、いろいろな場面の設定になっている。

⑧ Discussion Questions

最後の問題として、クラス内での話し合いに使える話題を2つ用意してある。当該単元に関連した身近な話題が提示してあるので、短く簡単な英語で自分の考えを表現してみる、というのがねらいである。（ご指導の先生方へ：クラスによっては宿題として、話すことを次回までに考えておくというスタンスでもよいと思われる。この話し合いの課題は、人数や時間などクラス設定との兼ね合いから、用途に応じて柔軟に扱うのがよいと考えられる。）

NHK NEWSLINE 6

CONTENTS

UNIT 01

Invention Needed: The Sillier the Better

「くだらないものグランプリ」

INVENTIONS NEEDED: THE SILLIER THE BETTER

放送日 2021/11/11

「くだらないものグランプリ」という大会が開かれた。コロナ禍で活気のない世の中を元気にしようと2020年から始まった。今回は愛知県小牧市の千成工業が作成した、おにぎりから苦手な具を抜き取る機械『グナッシ～』が優勝した。製品の有用性は限定的でも、町工場が培った技術は確かなものと、大会への評価は高い。

Words & Phrases

 CD 02

以下の単語や熟語の音声を聞きながら発音に注意し、意味を確認しましょう。

- [ ] **gadget** （目新しい）装置、道具
- [ ] **ingenuity** 発明の才、創意
- [ ] **COVID-19** 新型コロナウイルス〈Corona, Virus, Disease, 2019 を組み合わせた造語〉
- [ ] **pandemic** パンデミック、世界的感染病
- [ ] to **cheer**〈someone〉**up** 〈人〉を元気づける
- [ ] to **weld** 〈金属など〉を溶接する
- [ ] **air duct** エアダクト、通風管
- [ ] **filling** 中身、（中に入っている）具
- [ ] **contraption** （珍しい）仕掛け
- [ ] to **come up with** ～を思いつく

  例文 The CEO *came up with* a way to use his workforce more efficiently.
  最高経営責任者は、労働力をもっと効果的に使う方法を思いついた。

- [ ] **expertise** 専門知識

  例文 Your *expertise* in AI will be very useful for our project team.
  人工知能に関するあなたの知識は、私たちのプロジェクトチームに大変役に立つでしょう。

- [ ] **trivial** 些細な、取るに足らない
- [ ] to **showcase** ～を売り出す、紹介する

以下は、歴史的な発明に関する問題です。下の枠内から適切な語彙を選び、空所に入れましょう。

	Inventor	Known for	Country
1	Johannes Gutenberg		Germany
2	Leonardo da Vinci	Flying machines	
3	Benjamin Franklin		U.S.
4		Steam engine (condenser)	Scotland
5	Edward Jenner		
6		Dynamite	
7		Telephone	U.S.
8		Electric lamp	
9	Karl Benz		Germany
10	Wilhelm Roentgen		
11		Airplane	U.S.
12	John Atanasoff et.al.		U.S.

Alexander Graham Bell   Alfred Nobel   James Watt   Thomas Edison
Wright brothers   Electronic digital computer   Lightning rod
Motor car (Petrol)   Printing press   Vaccination   X-ray
England   Germany   Italy   Sweden   U.S.

1st Viewing >> Watch the News

ニュースを見て、内容と合っているものは T 、違っているものは F を選びましょう。

1. An aim of the competition was for teams to invent silly gadgets.   T・F

2. More than 20 small companies participated in this year's contest.   T・F

3. A member of the winning team gained weight after eating a lot of rice.   T・F

1 ニュースをもう一度見て、各問の空所に入る適切な選択肢を a ～ c から選びましょう。

1. After working on the device for a couple of months, the team _____.

   a. had gotten tired of eating too much rice
   b. neatly removed the center
   c. tried using a new kind of sheet metal

2. This team decided to invent an *onigiri* filling remover because _____.

   a. one member disliked a filling
   b. most fillings are too salty
   c. rice balls are healthier without filling

3. The narrator says that some workers _____.

   a. suggested having a nationwide competition
   b. complained about not having enough time
   c. learned new skills or information through this contest

2 以下はニュースの概要です。空所に適切な単語を書き入れましょう。語頭の文字（群）は与えてあります。

Factory workers in Aichi Prefecture joined a contest to create (**s**   [1]) inventions. The contest was designed to (**c**   [2]) up people during the pandemic. A small factory with 13 (**e**   [3]) won the first prize. They designed a special device to (**re**   [4]) *onigiri* fillings which they don't like. Even though there was no need for this device, the team's (**cra**   [5]) was excellent, and such inventions may lead to the development of new products.

Listen to the News Story

CDの音声を聞いて、News Story の ❶～❼ の文中にある空所に適切な単語を書き入れましょう。音声は2回繰り返されます。

Anchor: Factory workers have been testing their wits against each other in an unusual competition. The aim is to create silly inventions that are clever but largely pointless **gadgets**.

❶ We (¹) (²) (³)

5   (⁴) (⁵) (⁶)

(⁷) and **ingenuity** of these engineers.

❶ すばらしい熟練の技を見ていきましょう

Worker: Using this opener, you can open bottles while social distancing.

Narrator: Workers at 19 small factories battle to create the silliest

10   inventions. ❷ These items are the result (¹)

(²) (³), (⁴)

(⁵) (⁶).

❷ 彼らの好奇心や熱意や創造力の

The contest was launched in Aichi Prefecture, home to a thriving manufacturing sector in 2020 during the **COVID-19 pandemic**. Participating factories want to **cheer** people **up**

15   through the power of invention.

Woman: (*She announced the winner.*) Congratulations.

Narrator: The first prize went to a factory with 13 employees in Aichi Prefecture. The company processes and **welds** sheet metal

20   to manufacture shelves, **air ducts** and machine tools. The prize-winning gadget takes out the fish or vegetable **filling** of an *onigiri* or rice ball.

This **contraption** can remove the *onigiri*'s filling, but neatly leaves some rice and the seaweed wrapping.

25   ❸ The idea was inspired by an incident (¹)

(²) (³) (⁴)

(⁵) (⁶).

❸ 会社で起こった

❹ One day the president bought *onigiri* (¹)

(²) (³) (⁴)

30   (⁵) (⁶) (⁷).

Although they were happy to get something to eat, one of the

❹ 残業をする彼の従業員たちのために

4

employees did not like the filling in his rice ball.

The staff **came up with** the idea of creating a tool that can remove it. The team has **expertise** with sheet metal. ❺ But even so, (¹) (²) (³) (⁴) (⁵) (⁶) (⁷). As they experimented, they ate lots of *onigiri*. And one of them put on five kilograms. After two months, they could create highly accurate parts for their invention.

Hori Takayuki (Sennari Industry): ❻ It's able to cleanly (¹) (²) (³) (⁴) (⁵) (⁶) (⁷). The reason why it's silly is that if you don't like the filling, you can just eat a plain rice ball.

Narrator: The purpose of the competition was to create silly inventions. But for some companies, it was an unexpected opportunity to acquire new knowledge.

Man: ❼ Through the project, I was able to develop skills (¹) (²) (³) (⁴) (⁵) (⁶).

Woman: Staff fairly new to the company and with no manufacturing experience were able to participate.

Narrator: Members of the winning team say they realized the importance of carrying through with an idea, even if it seems **trivial**.

Kimura Shoji (Senior Managing Director, Sennari Industry): Everyone agreed it's important to pursue silly ideas. Otherwise, manufacturing would be no fun and technology would never improve.

Narrator: These silly inventions **showcase** the superb craftmanship of the manufacturing sector that may even lead to the development of new products. In the meantime, they are stimulating the employees' creativity and imagination.

❺ あまりよく知らないも
のを創り出すのは難し
い

❻ ご飯をあまりむだにせ
ずに、具を取り除く

❼ 以前使ったことがな
かった

各問、選択肢から適切な単語を選び、英文を完成させましょう。なお、余分な単語が１語ずつあります。

1. そのボランティアたちには、病院のみんなを歌で元気づけたいというしぜんな気持ちがあった。

   The volunteers (　　　　　　) a (　　　　　　) (　　　　　　) to
   (　　　　　　) (　　　　　　) everyone in the (　　　　　　) (　　　　　　)
   their songs.

with	had	desire	cheer	natural	hospital	down	up

2. たとえ完全に理解できなくても、他の宗教や文化をもつ人を尊重することは大切である。

   It's important (　　　　　　) (　　　　　　) (　　　　　　) with different
   (　　　　　　) and cultures, (　　　　　　) (　　　　　　) you don't
   (　　　　　　) understand them.

completely	to	people	how	even	respect	if	religions

3. 私たちは渋滞に巻き込まれたんです。そうでなければずっと前に来れたんですけど。

   We (　　　　　　) (　　　　　　) in a traffic (　　　　　　). (　　　　　　),
   we would (　　　　　　) (　　　　　　) much (　　　　　　).

earlier	got	catch	jam	have	arrived	stuck	otherwise

4. さ来週学年末試験をやりますので、その間に今学期学習した語彙を復習しておいてください。

   I will give the final exam the (　　　　　　) (　　　　　　) next. (　　　　　　)
   the (　　　　　　), (　　　　　　) all the vocabulary we (　　　　　　) studied
   this (　　　　　　).

review	in	term	week	were	meantime	after	have

1. Think of a useful invention which is impossible now but may be possible in 100 years. How could it change society or daily life?

2. Think of a sports game or award ceremony you saw. Who won a top prize? Why was it memorable?

6

UNIT 02

Artisan from Abroad Protects Tradition

筑前琵琶——イタリア人職人の思い

ARTISAN FROM ABROAD PROTECTS TRADITION

ドリアーノ・スリスさんは、筑前琵琶の作製・修復の職人で、福岡のイタリア会館館長も務める。若いとき琵琶に出合い、その独特な音色と形に強く魅了された。その後弟子入りし5年間修業を積んだ。現在も現役の筑前琵琶職人として日々仕事に励みながら、日本への感謝を示すため伝統技の継承にも力を入れている。

放送日 2021/4/2

Words & Phrases

◎ CD 04

以下の単語や熟語の音声を聞きながら発音に注意し、意味を確認しましょう。

☐ **artisan**　　　　　　（特に伝統工芸などの）職人
☐ **stringed instrument**　　弦楽器
☐ to **face**　　　　　～に直面する
☐ **craftsmanship**　　　（職人の）技能
☐ to **fascinate**　　　　～を魅了する
　例文 He was *fascinated* by Okinawan culture and traditions.
　　　彼は沖縄の文化や伝統に魅了された。
☐ **disciple**　　　　　弟子、門弟
☐ **maestro**　　　　　（芸術などの）巨匠、大家
☐ **apprentice**　　　　見習い、徒弟
☐ **cerebral**　　　　　大脳の
☐ **hemorrhage**　　　　出血
☐ to **die out**　　　　すたれる、絶滅する
☐ **intent**　　　　　　専念している、夢中になっている
　例文 Our new boss is *intent* on pleasing everyone.
　　　新しい上司はみんなを喜ばせようと努めている。

Before You Watch

以下は、音楽の感想を言うときに使える表現です。下の枠内から適切な単語を選び、空所に入れましょう。

1. The drummers' performance is very (　　　　　　　). かっこいい

2. The melody of this pop song is (　　　　　　). 美しい

3. Easy listening music is (　　　　　). 落ち着く

4. The folk song is (　　　　). 懐かしい

5. This hard rock music is (　　　　　). ワクワクする

6. This type of music makes me feel (　　　　　). 陰鬱な

7. Singing in a chorus is (　　　　　). 楽しい

8. Many types of music on TikTok are (　　　　　　). 陽気な[ノリがいい]

9. I love music with a (　　　　). 速度が速い

10. The Beatles' music is (　　　　　). すばらしい[すごい]

awesome/great　　beautiful　　cheerful/upbeat
comforting/relaxing　　cool　　depressed/sad　　enjoyable/fun
exciting/exhilarating　　fast tempo　　nostalgic

Watch the News

1st Viewing

ニュースを見て、内容と合っているものはT、違っているものはFを選びましょう。

1. The Chikuzen biwa originated in western Japan. T・F

2. Sulis was paid to learn how to play the Japanese instrument. T・F

3. Sulis was admitted to a hospital because he was injured in a car accident. T・F

1 ニュースをもう一度見て、各問の空所に入る適切な選択肢を a ～ c から選びましょう。

1. The Chikuzen biwa was played over 100 years ago, _____.

   a. and is still very popular among women

   b. but is not very popular anymore

   c. but is not played by men now

2. Sulis first heard the Chikuzen biwa being played _____.

   a. when he was in Japan

   b. during a TV concert

   c. less than 35 years ago

3. Sulis thinks _____ is important.

   a. passing on traditional manufacturing and repair skills

   b. manufacturing new types of musical instruments

   c. repeating the identical technique again and again

2 右の文字列を並べ替えて単語を作り、各文の空所に入れて意味がとおるようにしましょう。

1. The Chikuzen biwa is known for its (   ) and soft tone. [lhtig]

2. Sulis learned how to repair the instruments as a (   ) of his master. [deiplcis]

3. Sulis (   )ed from a health problem two years ago. [roveerc]

4. Sulis wants to hand down the (   ) to future generations. [cfatr]

Listen to the News Story

CD の音声を聞いて、News Story の ❶～❼ の文中にある空所に適切な単語を書き入れましょう。音声は 2 回繰り返されます。

Anchor: A **stringed instrument** traditional to one region of Japan is **facing** an uncertain future. ❶ Today there are very few people who know (　　　　　¹⁾ (　　　　　　²⁾ (　　　　　³⁾ (　　　　　⁴⁾ (　　　　　⁵⁾ (　　　　　⁶⁾ (　　　　　⁷⁾. One of the last is an artisan from abroad who's working to keep alive this musical tradition and its **craftsmanship**.

❶ どのようにして、これらの楽器を作ったり直したりするか

Narrator: The Chikuzen biwa is a small musical instrument traditional to western Japan, that is popular for its light and soft tone. More than 100 years ago, it was played widely, especially by women. But its popularity has gradually faded.

Doriano Sulis was born in Italy. He is a traditional Chikuzen biwa artisan. He first heard the instrument on the radio while visiting Japan 45 years ago. He says it changed the direction of his life.

Doriano Sulis (Chikuzen biwa artisan): ❷ It was (　　　　　¹⁾ (　　　　　²⁾ (　　　　　³⁾ (　　　　　⁴⁾ (　　　　　⁵⁾ (　　　　　⁶⁾ with a very mysterious tone. It **fascinated** me.

❷ それまで聞いたこともない楽器

Narrator: Even though he spoke little Japanese, Sulis became a **disciple** of Chikuzen biwa **maestro**, Yoshizuka Genzaburo. He was an unpaid **apprentice** for five years.

Sulis: This wood is very hard. The way these parts are inserted is quite complicated. ❸ (　　　　　¹⁾ (　　　　　²⁾ (　　　　　³⁾ (　　　　　⁴⁾ (　　　　　⁵⁾ (　　　　　⁶⁾. They're not all the same. I don't simply repeat the same thing again and again. Each time I craft a new instrument. I never get tired of doing this. I love it.

❸ 各々の職人が自分独自の技術を持っている

Narrator: Two years ago, Sulis was hospitalized after suffering a **cerebral hemorrhage**, but he recovered.

10

Sulis: I feel deeply that I must pass on this craft. ❹ I'm not young any more, (　　　　　　 1) (　　　　　　 2) (　　　　 3) (　　　　　 4) (　　　　　 5) (　　　　 6) (　　　　　 7).

5 **Narrator:** This winter Sulis took on his first apprentice. It is important to him that the traditional skills live on.

Sulis: (*While working on a Chikuzen biwa*) The whole thing needs to fit in perfectly. Just this much, a little at a time. Don't take off too much.

10 **Gondo Satomi** (*Chikuzen biwa apprentice*)**:** ❺ I've always (　　　　　　 1) (　　　 2) (　　　　 3) (　　　　 4) (　　　 5) (　　　　　 6). There's so much to learn. It's both exciting and fun.

Sulis: It would be terrible if this wonderful instrument were to 15 **die out**. ❻ I want to give back to Japan (　　　　　 1) (　　　 2) (　　　　 3) (　　　　 4) (　　　 5).

Narrator: ❼ Sulis is **intent** on ensuring that the beautiful music of the Chikuzen biwa will continue (　　　　 1) 20 (　　　 2) (　　　　 3) (　　　　 4) (　　　 5) (　　　　 6) (　　　　 7).

---

❹ それで、あまり時間が 残っていない

❺ 伝統的な日本の技術に 興味があった

❻ ここで学んだすべての こと

❼ 将来長く演奏される ［聴かれる］

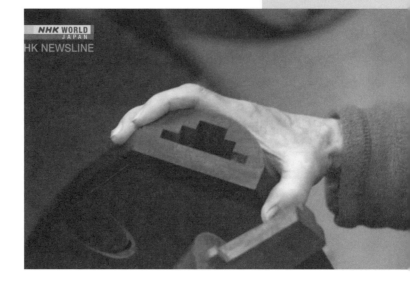

各問、選択肢から適切な単語を選び、英文を完成させましょう。なお、余分な単語が1語
ずつあります。

1. 節約しようとしているんだけど、来る日も来る日も同じ安物の即席麺を食べるのは飽きた。

I'm trying to (　　　　　) (　　　　　　　　) , but I (＿＿＿＿＿＿) (＿＿＿＿＿)
(＿＿＿＿＿＿) eating the same (　　　　　　) instant noodles day after
(　　　　　).

| tired | tomorrow | of | cheap | money | got | day | save |

2. ティントレットは、彼の絵画技術とアートスタジオを息子たちに継承した。

Tintoretto (＿＿＿＿＿＿) (＿＿＿＿＿＿) his (　　　　　) (　　　　　) and
(　　　　) (　　　　　) (　　　　　　) his sons.

| to | passed | art | painting | composed | studio | techniques | on |

3. この図書館の唯一の問題点は、一度に5冊以上 [を超えて] 借りられないことである。

The only problem (　　　　　) this (　　　　　　) is that people
(　　　　　) borrow (　　　　　) (　　　　　　) five books (＿＿＿＿＿＿)
a (＿＿＿＿＿).

| more | with | can't | time | at | fewer | than | library |

4. 恐竜は6600万年前に絶滅したので、人間には一度も遭遇していない。

Dinosaurs (＿＿＿＿＿＿) (＿＿＿＿＿) 66 (　　　　　) years ago and,
(　　　　　), never (　　　　　) (　　　　　) (　　　　　　).

| out | million | beings | encountered | therefore | human | with | died |

1. What kind of musical instruments do you like best? Why?

2. Would you be interested in learning to make or play the Chikuzen biwa? Why or
why not?

UNIT 03

World Traveler, Starting by Accident

世界をつなぐ音吉

SHIPWRECK SURVIVOR INSPIRES GLOBAL VISION

放送日 2021/10/4

音吉は愛知県美浜町出身で、地元では日本最初の国際人とも言われる。彼は1832年仲間と共に廻船で江戸へ向かう途中、嵐に遭い太平洋を漂流した。英語の書物の翻訳に従事し、中国で日本人漂流民たちの援助を行い、通訳として日英交渉に尽力した。美浜町は音吉の活躍や当時の生活の様子を積極的に海外に発信しており、シンガポールとの友好関係も深まっている。

Words & Phrases

◎ CD 06

以下の単語や熟語の音声を聞きながら発音に注意し、意味を確認しましょう。

- ☐ shipwreck　　難破
- ☐ survivor　　生存者
- ☐ adrift　　漂流して
  - 例文 John Mung's ship went *adrift* in 1841 because of a typhoon.
    ジョン万次郎の船は、1841年に台風で漂流した。
- ☐ dedicated to　　〜にささげられた
- ☐ maritime　　海洋の
- ☐ to be descended from　　〜の子孫である
  - 例文 He claims that he *is descended from* a famous samurai.
    彼は有名な武士の子孫だと主張している。
- ☐ crew　　船乗り
- ☐ globetrotter　　世界を駆けまわる人
- ☐ aviation　　飛行術

以下は、旅行の宿泊に関する表現です。下の枠内から適切な単語を選び、空所に入れましょう。

1. 「山﨑」という名前で予約しています。

   I have a (　　　　　) (　　　　　　) the name, Yamazaki.

2. シングルルーム1泊で予約をしています。

   I (　　　　　) a single room for one night.

3. 明日7時にモーニングコール、お願いできますか。

   Could you (　　　　　) me a (　　　　　) call tomorrow morning at 7:00?

4. 今晩空いている部屋はありますか。

   Do you have (　　　　　) rooms (　　　　　) for tonight?

5. 部屋を締め出されてしまいました。

   I accidentally (　　　　　) (　　　　　) (　　　　　).

6. 隣の部屋がうるさいです。

   The (　　　　　) next door are (　　　　　).

7. お湯が出ません。　There's (　　　　　) (　　　　　) (　　　　　).

8. もう1泊できますか。

   Can I (　　　　　) my (　　　　　) for one (　　　　　) night?

9. チェックアウトの後、荷物を預かっていただけますか。

   (　　　　　) you (　　　　　) my (　　　　　) after I check out?

10. タクシーを呼んでください。　Please (　　　　　) a (　　　　　) for me.

any	available	booked	call	could	extend	give	guests
hold	hot	locked	luggage	more	myself	no	noisy	out
reservation	stay	taxi	under	wake-up	water

ニュースを見て、内容と合っているものは T 、違っているものは F を選びましょう。

1. As a young teenager, Otokichi worked as a sailor. 　T・F

2. Otokichi was working on translating Shakespeare's dramas into Japanese. 　T・F

3. Lim had known a lot about Otokichi before she came to Mihama to work. 　T・F

1 ニュースをもう一度見て、各問の空所に入る適切な選択肢を a ~ c から選びましょう。

1. After drifting in a ship, Otokichi finally reached _____.

   a. a desert island in the Pacific Ocean
   b. the West Coast of the United States
   c. the town of Mihama in Aichi Prefecture

2. Otokichi _____.

   a. wrote books in Singapore
   b. returned to Japan as an interpreter
   c. never came back to Japan

3. Lim is interested in _____.

   a. translating information about Otokichi into English
   b. erecting a statue of Otokichi in Singapore
   c. building a new museum in Mihama

2 ニュースに関して、空所に入る適切な数字を枠内から選びましょう（余分な選択肢があります）。

1. Otokichi traveled the world for about (　　　　　　) years.

2. Otokichi's ship sailed off course when he was (　　　　　　).

3. The museum dedicated to Otokichi is a house built (　　　　　　) years ago.

4. Otokichi passed away when he was around (　　　　　　).

12	14	25	35	50	100	150	250	300

Listen to the News Story

CDの音声を聞いて、News Story の ❶〜❼ の文中にある空所に適切な単語を書き入れましょう。音声は2回繰り返されます。

Anchor: Next, the story of a Japanese **shipwreck survivor** two
centuries ago is being retold at home and abroad. Otokichi
traveled the globe for 35 years, never to return. ❶ As we'll see
in our next report, (¹) (²)

5　　(³) (⁴) (⁵)
(⁶) (⁷) in memory of its
native son.

❶ 彼の生誕の地が今、国際的関係を促進している

Narrator: ❷ Otokichi was already a sailor at the age of 14,
(¹) (²) (³)

10　　(⁴) (⁵) (⁶)
he was aboard **adrift**. He was pushed across the Pacific
Ocean and finally washed ashore on the West Coast of
the United States. ❸ It was the 1830s, and Japan was
(¹) (²) (³)

15　　(⁴) (⁵) (⁶)
(⁷). Unable to return home, Otokichi
traveled the globe instead.

❷ 嵐が来て船を転覆させた時

❸ 世界のほとんどの地域に門を閉ざしていた

He was involved in the first translation of the *Bible*
into Japanese. ❹ It came in some years later as

20　　(¹) (²) (³)
(⁴) (⁵) (⁶)
(⁷). A museum **dedicated to** Otokichi is
located in a remodeled, 250-year-old Japanese house.

❹ その国が外国に対して門戸を開き始めた

Higuchi Hirohisa (Otokichi Kinenkan): I wanted to preserve what little is left from

25　　that era to teach people about life 200 years ago.

Narrator: Higuchi spent six years working with the community to
gather material about its **maritime** culture. He himself **is
descended from** the owner of the shipwrecked boat. Unlike
Otokichi, most of the **crew** didn't survive.

30　**Higuchi:** I'm sorry many people died when the ship ended up adrift.

Narrator: (*An elementary school class is shown.*) ❺ Otokichi's story

❺ この女性のおかげもあって

16

is reaching people around the world, (¹)
(²) (³) (⁴)
(⁵) (⁶). Lim Yi Xuan was
invited to Mihama from Singapore to promote relations
with that country. Before coming to work in Mihama, she
didn't know about Otokichi, his travels or his last years in
Singapore. He was a **globe trotter** long before **aviation**
made that possible for most people.

Lim Yi Xuan (Mihama International Relations Coordinator): ❻ (¹)
(²) (³) (⁴)
(⁵) (⁶) Otokichi and
Mihama is in Japanese. ❼ I want to translate it into
English and (¹) (²)
(³) (⁴) (⁵)
(⁶).

Thanks to Otokichi, Mihama and Singapore have a historical
relationship. I hope to continue building on that.

Narrator: Otokichi died in Singapore at around the age of 50. With the
help of Lim, his story is becoming known, as one for the ages.

❻ 〜についてのオンライ
ン情報のほとんどすべ
てが〜

❼ その物語を世界に知ら
せる

各問、選択肢から適切な単語を選び、英文を完成させましょう。なお、余分な単語が1語ずつあります。

1. 修士論文を書いているときに、最も大事なファイルの一つを誤って削除してしまった。

    When I (   ) (   ) (   ) my (   ) , I
    (   ) one of my most important files (_____) (_____).

accident	working	by	on	detected	thesis	deleted	was

2. 電車の線路に落ちた日本人を助けようとして死亡した韓国の学生を偲んで、法要が行われた。

    A (   ) was (   ) in (_____) (_____) a
    Korean student (   ) died (   ) to help a Japanese that had
    (   ) on the train tracks.

of	service	trying	memory	who	fallen	picked	held

3. 将来、国際貿易に関係のある仕事に携わりたい。

    (   ) the (   ) , I would like to (_____) (_____)
    in work (   ) to (   ) (   ).

trade	in	hold	related	future	be	international	involved

4. 良い友達のおかげで、何か月も探してやっとこの素敵なアパートを見つけた。

    (_____) (_____) a good friend of (   ) , I finally
    (   ) this nice apartment (   ) (   ) for
    (   ).

months	to	thanks	after	because	mine	searching	found

1. If you were given one year of time off from school or work, where would you go or what would you do during that time? Why?

2. Otokichi lived in the Edo period. If you had a choice, what period would you like to live in? Why?

UNIT 04

International Volunteers Help Children in Need

国際子ども食堂

INTERNATIONAL VOLUNTEERS HELP CHILDREN IN NEED

「こども食堂」という言葉をよく聞くようになった。子どもたちに対し無料あるいは格安で栄養バランスのとれた食事が提供される。さらに親どうしのコミュニケーションがとれるというメリットもある。一方、運営には課題も多くボランティアや寄付などの支援も必要となる。多文化共生を軸にしている愛媛の例をレポートする。

放送日 2021/5/31

Words & Phrases

◎ CD 08

以下の単語や熟語の音声を聞きながら発音に注意し、意味を確認しましょう。

☐ **volunteer-run** ボランティアによる運営の
☐ to **spring up** 立ち上がる、現れる
例文 New business buildings have *sprung up* like mushrooms in the metropolitan area.
新しいビジネス建築が、首都圏にキノコのように現れた。
☐ to **interact** with 〜と触れ合う、交流する
☐ to **treat** 〈人〉をもてなす
☐ to **set up** 〜を開設する、立ち上げる
☐ **coronavirus** 新型コロナウイルス
☐ **outbreak** 発生、勃発
例文 People were shocked by the sudden *outbreak* of monkeypox in several countries.
人々は、サル痘の突然の発生にショックを受けた。
☐ **therapy** セラピー、治療

Before You Watch

以下は、語源に関する問題です。下の選択肢から日本語を選び表の空所に入れましょう。

	語彙	意味	形態素	意味	形態素	意味	形態素	意味
(例)	**international**	国際的な	**inter-**	〜の間の	**-nation-**	国家	**-al**	〜の
1	pandemic	世界的伝染病	pan-		-dem-	民衆	-ic	〜のような
2	coronavirus	コロナウイルス	corona		-virus	ウイルス		
3	ecology		eco-	家の	-logy			
4	bilingual	バイリンガルの	bi-		-lingua-		-al	〜の
5	introduction	紹介	intro-		-duct-		-tion	こと
6	predict		pre-		-dict			
7	import	輸入する	im-	中に	-port			
8	confidence	自信	con-		-fid-		-ence	こと
9	exclusive		ex-		-clus-		-ive	
10	associate	交際する	as-	〜のほうへ	-soci-		-ate	

> 言う　　学問　　完全に　　冠　　言語　　事前に　　社会
> 信じる　　すべての　　〜する　　生態学　　外へ　　閉じる　　中に
> 〜のような　　排他的な　　運ぶ　　2つの　　導く　　予言する

1st Viewing >> Watch the News

ニュースを見て、内容と合っているものは T 、違っているものは F を選びましょう。

1. Volunteer-run cafeterias are needed very much now all over Japan.　　T・F

2. Sofia came to Japan a few years ago to work for a Japanese company.　　T・F

3. Sofia felt lonely in Japan after the coronavirus epidemic began.　　T・F

2nd Viewing >> Understand the News

1 ニュースをもう一度見て、各問の空所に入る適切な選択肢を a ~ c から選びましょう。

1. In Matsuyama City, international meals are served _____.

   a. every day
   b. once a week
   c. on special occasions

2. Sofia once volunteered to cook _____.

   a. curry for 20 people
   b. Japanese food for 30 students
   c. ethnic food for 40 visitors

3. Yamase says that it is beneficial for children to _____.

   a. interact with people from different parts of the world
   b. find out more about local fisheries in Ehime
   c. learn how the coronavirus spreads worldwide

2 以下はニュースの概要です。空所に適切な単語を書き入れましょう。語頭の文字（群）が与えてあるものもあります。

Cafeterias run by (**v**   ¹)《複数形》 are popular in Japan. These places provide (**m**   ²)《複数形》 for children in need. Children also have chances to play with staff members. This (**in**   ³) cafeteria in Ehime has university student helper participants from Europe, Africa and Asia. Sofia came to Japan from (⁴) to study. But her classes were soon offered (**on**   ⁵) due to COVID-19. She felt lonely, until she was invited to participate in this program and (**c**   ⁶) food with the children. She enjoys talking and playing with the kids.

Listen to the News Story

CDの音声を聞いて、News Story の ❶～❼ の文中にある空所に適切な単語を書き入れましょう。音声は2回繰り返されます。

Anchor: A network of more than 5,000 **volunteer-run** cafeterias has **sprung up** across Japan in recent years to provide meals for children who are not getting enough to eat. One that opened in the southwestern prefecture of Ehime is also giving children a chance to **interact with** visitors from other countries.

Narrator: (*At the children's cafeteria*) It's 4 p.m. That's the time when the children start to arrive at the international children's cafeteria in Matsuyama City. ❶ They come here to eat, but they also (¹) (²) (³) (⁴) (⁵) (⁶) (⁷). ❷ Today they (¹) (²) (³) (⁴) (⁵) (⁶) (⁷).

All: *Itadakimasu.*

Narrator: Since March of this year, meals like this have been served once a week, prepared by students from countries across Europe, Africa and Asia. ❸ Of course, (¹) (²) (³) (⁴) (⁵) (⁶) (⁷). This project was **set up** by Yamase Marie.

Yamase Marie (Founder, International children's cafeteria)**:** ❹ I wanted to create a place (¹) (²) (³) (⁴) (⁵) (⁶) (⁷). Some visiting students told me they'd like to prepare some dishes from their home countries.

Narrator: Sofia Mateen is from India. She comes to the cafeteria every week. ❺ For her, interacting with the children and others is a way (¹) (²) (³) (⁴) (⁵) (⁶).

❶ ボランティアスタッフと遊ぶようになる

❷ ベトナムの食事をごちそうになる

❸ 厳しい感染管理の手段が用意された

❹ 多くの人がくつろげる（場所）

❺ 日本文化を、より身近に感じる

Reporter: How do you like playing with the children?

Sofia Mateen (Student): It's fun. I love it.

Narrator: Sofia arrived in Ehime two years ago. ❻ From the start,
she enjoyed her university studies and (¹)
(²) (³) (⁴)
(⁵) (⁶). But things changed
following the **coronavirus outbreak** in Japan. ❼ Classes
were moved online, and she found herself (¹)
(²) (³) (⁴)
(⁵) (⁶) in her apartment.

Mateen: The *corona*[*virus*] was not there when I first came to Japan.
So I thought life *will* be very fun and very easy, ah, in
Matsuyama, and I *can*[*1] enjoy as well as (*I can*[*2]) study. I
can[*1] do my study.

Narrator: Being away from her family for over a year and a half, she
started feeling homesick. That's when she heard Yamase was
inviting volunteers to help her in the cafeteria. One time she
prepared a meal for 40 people, an Indian chicken curry.

Mateen: We play, eat and cook together. It's fun, almost like **therapy**.

Yamase: There will be more and more international students and
foreigners visiting Ehime. If the children interact with many
different people when they are young, that will make it easier
for them when they are grown up. I want to make this a place
where anyone from any country can come and feel at home.

Narrator: Even during the pandemic, the success of this international
children's cafeteria can be seen in the smiles on the faces of
the children and the volunteers from abroad. Kimura Miyako,
NHK World.

❻ 友だちとの社会生活も
…

❼ 一人で過ごす時間が
もっと多くなった

Notes:（p. 23）ℓ. 12　corona に続けて virus が必要

　　　　　ℓ. 13　この場合 will は文法的には would を使うのが正しい

　　　　　ℓ. 14 [*1]　この場合 can は文法的には could を使うのが正しい

　　　　　ℓ. 14 [*2]　I can は削除する必要がある

各問、選択肢から適切な単語を選び、英文を完成させましょう。なお、余分な単語が1語
ずつあります。

1. 加奈は大学に入って間もないけれど、寮の仲間とはうまく付き合っている。

   (＿＿＿＿＿＿＿) Kana is (＿＿＿＿＿＿＿) to the university, she (＿＿＿＿＿＿＿) well
   (＿＿＿＿＿＿＿) the (＿＿＿＿＿＿＿) (＿＿＿＿＿＿＿) in her (＿＿＿＿＿＿＿).

   | dormitory | interacts | although | new | residents | another | with | other |

2. いろいろな環境問題に取り組むために専門家の助けを得て、委員会が立ち上げられた。

   With the (＿＿＿＿＿＿＿) of (＿＿＿＿＿＿＿), a panel was (＿＿＿＿＿＿＿)
   (＿＿＿＿＿＿＿) to (＿＿＿＿＿＿＿) various (＿＿＿＿＿＿＿) (＿＿＿＿＿＿＿).

   | set | help | experts | outsiders | problems | tackle | up | environmental |

3. もしよく知らない人たちとアパートをシェアしなければいけないなら、香織は東京でくつろげ
   ることはないだろう。

   Kaori would never (＿＿＿＿＿＿＿) (＿＿＿＿＿＿＿) (＿＿＿＿＿＿＿) in Tokyo, if
   she (＿＿＿＿＿＿＿) to (＿＿＿＿＿＿＿) an apartment with (＿＿＿＿＿＿＿) she
   (＿＿＿＿＿＿＿) know very well.

   | comfortable | home | didn't | feel | share | at | had | people |

4. 私は自分たちの新興企業がそんなわずかな資本金で成功するのか、最初から疑問に思った。

   (＿＿＿＿＿＿＿) the (＿＿＿＿＿＿＿), I (＿＿＿＿＿＿＿) if our start-up
   (＿＿＿＿＿＿＿) be (＿＿＿＿＿＿＿) with so (＿＿＿＿＿＿＿) (＿＿＿＿＿＿＿).

   | capital | wondered | successful | would | from | capitol | start | little |

Discussion Questions

1. What are the advantages and disadvantages of offering volunteer-run cafeterias for children in need? Explain.

2. Have you participated in any community activities? If yes, what kind? How were they? If no, why not?

Public Servant Goes Private

UNIT 05

買い物難民を救え——元官僚、IT 企業へ

自動配送ロボットで「買い物難民」を救いたいという大きな目標を掲げる人がいる。牛嶋裕之氏は現在楽天グループに属し、無人配送ソリューションを提供する事業部で、ロボットが荷物を届けるサービスの開発を担当している。既に横須賀市で実施し良い感触を得ており、過去の物流システムを変える大きなプロジェクトに期待が寄せられている。

放送日 2021/5/11

Words & Phrases

CD 10

以下の単語や熟語の音声を聞きながら発音に注意し、意味を確認しましょう。

☐ **public servant** 公務員

☐ **disrupter** ディスラプター、創造的破壊者〈デジタル技術を使い従来の方法やサービスを効率の良いものに変える人や企業〉

☐ **hungry** 野心的な、やる気のある

例文 Many young people are *hungry* for jobs these days.
最近多くの若者が仕事をほしがっている。

☐ **dropout** 退学者

☐ **bureaucrat** 官僚

☐ **autonomous** 自律性の

☐ **staff** [stǽf] スタッフ〈cf., stuff [stʌ́f]「もの」、との発音の違いに注意〉

例文 Kaito worked as a member of the volunteer cleaning *staff* at the park.
海斗はボランティア清掃スタッフとして、その公園で働いた。

☐ **Ministry of Economy, Trade and Industry** [METI] 経済産業省

☐ **subsidy** 助成金、補助金

☐ **simultaneously** 同時に

以下は、車や道路関係の英語表現です。下の枠内から適切な単語［米語］を選び、空所に入れましょう。

1. 事故が起きたとき私が運転していた。

   I was (　　　　　　) the (　　　　　　　　) at the time of the accident.

2. スピード違反をしていたので、路肩に止めさせられた。

   I was told to (　　　　　　) (　　　　　　　　) because I was (　　　　　　).

3. 車がパンクした。

   My car has a (　　　　　　) (　　　　　　).

4. その有名人はひき逃げの容疑をかけられた。

   The celebrity was (　　　　　　) with a (　　　　　　) accident.

5. 彼は信号無視の歩行者にクラクションを鳴らした。

   He honked his (　　　　　　) at the (　　　　　　).

6. ハイウェイで交通渋滞に巻き込まれた。

   I was (　　　　　　) in a traffic (　　　　　　) on the (　　　　　　).

7. バックミラーを見ると、後ろに救急車が見えた。

   When I looked in my (　　　　　　) mirror, I saw an (　　　　　　) behind us.

8. まっすぐ行って、信号を左折してください。

   Go (　　　　　　) down this road and (　　　　　　) left at the (　　　　　　) light.

ambulance	behind	caught	charged	flat	freeway
hit-and-run	horn	jam	jaywalker	over	pull	rearview
speeding	straight	tire	traffic	turn	wheel

ニュースを見て、内容と合っているものは T 、違っているものは F を選びましょう。

1. The autonomous robot can sense obstacles more than 50 meters away.　T・F

2. This robot is expected to help elderly people who can't go grocery shopping.　T・F

3. One person watching a single robot is a good use of personnel.　T・F

1 ニュースをもう一度見て、各問の空所に入る適切な選択肢を a ~ c から選びましょう。

1. A couple of years ago, Ushijima _____.

    a. started his career as a bureaucrat

    b. was transferred to a new department at METI

    c. ended his work for the government

2. When companies started using robots in their facilities, Ushijima _____.

    a. did not hear about the news

    b. was enjoying his bureaucratic duties

    c. became interested in this kind of work

3. At the IT company, Ushijima _____.

    a. negotiated with government ministries

    b. began to doubt the usefulness of using robots

    c. paid more attention to younger workers

2 右の文字列を並べ替えて単語を作り、各文の空所に入れて意味がとおるようにしましょう。語頭の文字（群）は与えてあります。

1. A (**bu**   ) is an official in a government department.   [ratureac]

2. This robot vehicle is useful for delivering groceries to old people or (**s**   )s.

                                                         [reino]

3. A college (**d**   ) is a person who has given up a course of study at college.   [utporo]

4. A (**t**   ) run of the robot vehicle was done on a regular road.   [lrai]

Listen to the News Story

CDの音声を聞いて、News Story の ❶〜❼ の文中にある空所に適切な単語を書き入れましょう。音声は2回繰り返されます。

Anchor: When you think of an industry **disrupter**, you might be picturing a young and **hungry** college **dropout**, but in Japan some of the freshest ideas are coming from a surprising place, former **bureaucrats**.

5 (*Rakuten robot talks.*) "All clear. Let's go!"

Narrator: ❶ An **autonomous** (¹) (²) (³) (⁴) (⁵) (⁶) (⁷). It's the first time such a trial project has been carried out on a public road in

10 Japan.

The robot uses sensors and cameras to detect obstacles up to 30 meters away. The idea is to help seniors who can't go shopping and to deal with shortages of delivery **staff**.

Man: How is the service?

15 **Woman:** It's convenient. I'm grateful it comes straight to my door.

Narrator: Ushijima Hiroyuki is the leader of the project. ❷ He worked for the **Ministry of Economy, Trade and Industry** (¹) (²) (³) (⁴) (⁵) (⁶).

20 One area of Ushijima's work involved regulations concerning **subsidies** for companies that develop robots. He quit his job at the Ministry two years ago. ❸ He decided he wanted to work for a company that was (¹) (²) (³) (⁴)

25 (⁵) (⁶).

Ushijima Hiroyuki (Senior Manager, UGV Business Section, Rakuten Group): When I heard about companies launching businesses using robots, I wanted to do it myself. ❹ I (¹) (²) (³) (⁴) (⁵)

30 (⁶) using them.

❶ ロボット車が商品をスーパーから配送する

❷ 彼がIT会社に加わる前に

❸ 社会問題に取り組むために何か行っている

❹ 事業とかサービスに興味を持つようになった

28

Narrator: He helped coordinate among government offices as they formulated policy. At the IT firm, Ushijima checks laws and regulations when he comes up against bureaucratic barriers. He tells relevant ministries or agencies about the need to reform them.

❺ One problem facing the company is that each robot

(¹) (²) (³)

(⁴) (⁵) (⁶)

(⁷). It's not a profitable business strategy. Having each monitor look after several robots **simultaneously** makes more sense.

Ushijima is compiling data to convince bureaucrats it's safe to do that.

Ushijima: A system can be revised only when there's a clear vision of what sort of merits a business or a service can bring.

❻ I want to (¹) (²)

(³) (⁴) (⁵)

(⁶).

Narrator: How soon can this new business meet growing public demand by getting more robots on the road? ❼ That

(¹) (²) (³)

(⁴) (⁵) (⁶)

of this former bureaucrat.

❺ 人、一人で監視されなければならない

❻ どのようにして社会に利益をもたらすことができるか示す

❼ 交渉力しだいかもしれない

各問、選択肢から適切な単語を選び、英文を完成させましょう。なお、余分な単語が 1 語ずつあります。

1. 私の祖母は長年、癌を患い亡くなった。母が祖母が亡くなるまでお世話をした。

   My grandmother (　　　　　　) (　　　　　　　) after (　　　　　　)
   from (　　　　　　) for many years. My mother (＿＿＿＿＿＿) (＿＿＿＿＿＿)
   her until her (　　　　　　).

took	after	death	passed	suffering	away	looked	cancer

2. この使用説明は私には意味がよくわかりません。（ちょっと）助けていただけますか。

   These (　　　　　　) don't (＿＿＿＿＿) much (＿＿＿＿＿) to
   (　　　　　　). Maybe you (　　　　　) (　　　　　) me (　　　　　).

could	directions	understand	make	sentence	me	help	sense

3. 日本は需要を満たすために、世界中から多くの商品を輸入する。

   Japan imports a (　　　　　) (　　　　　) (　　　　　) products
   (　　　　　) all (　　　　　) the world to (＿＿＿＿＿) (＿＿＿＿＿).

demand	under	from	number	over	large	of	meet

4. ジムはずいぶんバイトに時間を使っています。でも彼の将来は、今一生懸命勉強をするかどうかによって決まります。

   Jim (　　　　　) a (　　　　　) of time working (　　　　　). But his
   future (＿＿＿＿＿) (＿＿＿＿＿) (　　　　　) or (　　　　　) he
   studies hard now.

on	not	lot	depends	neither	spends	whether	part-time

Discussion Questions

1. Do you think it is a good idea to use robots to deliver merchandise from supermarkets? Why?

2. What are the advantages and disadvantages of using robots at a restaurant? Explain.

Hiroshima Hibakusha Determined to Share Story

英語を始めた被爆者

HIROSHIMA HIBAKUSHA DETERMINED TO SHARE STORY

広島県府中町の八幡照子さんは、原爆が投下されたとき小学生だった。彼女は、船で世界を一周し各地の人々と交流する「ピースボート」に乗り寄港地で平和を訴える被爆者の一人だ。英語ができればもっと直接自分の被爆体験が共有できると実感し、高齢ながら学習を始めた。日々、被爆証言の活動に励む。

放送日 2021/4/21

Words & Phrases

 CD 12

以下の単語や熟語の音声を聞きながら発音に注意し、意味を確認しましょう。

- [ ] to **deprive** A **of** B　　A から B を奪う
- [ ] to **dim**　　〈感情など〉を弱める、薄める
- [ ] to **reach out**　　働きかける
- [ ] to **devastate**　　～を荒廃させる

例文 A massive volcanic eruption *devastated* the land.
火山の大噴火がその土地を荒廃させた。

- [ ] to **throw oneself into**　　～に打ち込む、熱心に身を投じる

例文 He *threw himself into* his work.
彼はその仕事に打ち込んだ。

- [ ] **blast**　　爆発
- [ ] **anguish**　　（心身の）激しい苦痛
- [ ] **testimonial**　　証明となる、証拠の
- [ ] **Peace Boat**　　ピースボート〈国際交流を目的に設立された日本の NGO、あるいはその団体が企画した船舶旅行〉
- [ ] **illegitimate**　　非合法の

Before You Watch

以下は、教師が教室で使う英語表現です。下の枠内から適切な単語を選び、空所に入れましょう。なお、余分な単語もあります。

1. 調子はどうですか。   How are (   ) going?

2. 出席を取ります。   I'll take (   ).

3. 〈出席を取られて〉はい。   (   ). / Present.

4. 今日は何曜日ですか。   (   ) (   ) is it today?

5. 今日は何日ですか。   What's today's (   )?

6. この前の授業を簡単に復習しましょう。
   Let's (   ) (   ) our last lesson.

7. 前に来て、黒板に答えを書いてください。
   Come up to the (   ) and write your answers on the board.

8. やってくれる人はいますか。手を挙げてください。
   Any (   )? (   ) your hands.

9. よくできました。   Well (   ). / You did a good (   ).

10. 各自、プリントを 1 枚取ってください。   Please take one (   ) each.

11. ペア／グループ、になってください。   Get into (   ) / groups.

12. レポートの締切りは来週です。   Your paper is (   ) next week.

13. 時間がなくなってきました。   We are (   ) (   ) of time.

14. 今日の授業は終わりにしましょう。
    Let's (   ) (   ) today's lesson.

attendance	date	day	done	due	fast	front	go
gone	handout	here	job	over	pairs	raise	rise
running	short	things	up	volunteers	what	wrap	

1st Viewing ≫ Watch the News

ニュースを見て、内容と合っているものは T 、違っているものは F を選びましょう。

1. Yahata was ten years old when the atomic bomb was dropped in Hiroshima.   T・F

2. Yahata's goal is to share her story with people around the world.   T・F

3. When Hiroshima was bombed in 1945, Yahata was at home with her family.   T・F

1 ニュースをもう一度見て、各問の空所に入る適切な選択肢を a ~ c から選びましょう。

1. When Yahata earnestly began talking about her war experience, she _____.

   a. had children at home
   b. worked in an office
   c. was over 70 years old

2. When Yahata was traveling around the world on the Peace Boat, she wished she had _____.

   a. better English communication skills
   b. started her peace activities sooner
   c. more experience as a public speaker

3. Yahata was encouraged to study English after _____.

   a. her mother protected her family during the bombing
   b. American troops began occupying Japan in 1945
   c. she heard Thurlow's speech about the importance of peace

2 以下の各情報を、ニュースに出てきた順序に並べましょう。

1. Yahata and all her family members survived the atomic bombing.

2. Yahata was impressed by the speech of a peace activist.

3. Yahata traveled around the world on the Peace Boat.

4. Yahata is practicing reading English aloud by herself.

Listen to the News Story

CDの音声を聞いて、News Story の ❶〜❼ の文中にある空所に適切な単語を書き入れましょう。音声は2回繰り返されます。

Anchor: Event cancellations during the pandemic *have* **deprived** survivors **of** the atomic bombings, or hibakusha, of regular opportunities to share their experiences. But as our next story shows, that hasn't **dimmed** the enthusiasm of one 83-year-old who is using the time to learn new skills to **reach out** to the world.

Yahata Teruko (Atomic bomb survivor): (*She reads.*) Memories of an eight-year-old *in* Hiroshima, 1945. Let's try one more time. Memories of....

Narrator: Yahata Teruko was eight years old when her hometown of Hiroshima was **devastated**. Now she's **throwing herself into** studying English with the aim of sharing her story outside of Japan.

Yahata Teruko: I didn't even know the word 'nuclear' in English....

It's quite challenging. ❶ I think I'll be (¹)
(²) (³) (⁴)
(⁵) (⁶) (⁷)
if I continue my studies.

❶ 英語で自分の考えを表現できる

Narrator: Yahata and her family were at home when the bomb was dropped. ❷ (¹) (²)
(³) (⁴) (⁵)
(⁶) (⁷), the family all survived. Fearing another **blast**, Yahata's mother covered everyone with a heavy futon for protection.

❷ 家屋はひどく被害を受けたが

Yahata: ❸ Even though I was young, I could (¹)
(²) (³) (⁴)
(⁵) (⁶) (⁷).
Still, I feel the **anguish** of war should never happen again.

❸ 家族の絆を本当に感じる

Narrator: Years later, with her own family grown and work behind her, Yahata finally began her **testimonial** activities in earnest when she passed 70.

34

She traveled the world on the **Peace Boat**, sharing her hibakusha experience. However, she felt being able to speak English would help her share even more.

5　Yahata was further encouraged to study after hearing a speech by peace activist Setsuko Thurlow.

Setsuko Thurlow (Atomic bomb survivor): ❹ ([1])

([2]) ([3]) ([4]),

([5]) ([6]) ([7]).

Change the world. Thank you.

10　*Yahata:*　❺ I got the feeling that I ([1])

([2]) ([3]) ([4])

([5]) ([6]) ([7]).

Narrator:　The Hiroshima Peace Memorial Museum translated part of Yahata's testimony into English. Now she's preparing to use

15　it in her future activities.

Yahata:　Who do you love? What do you want to protect? I want to put my heart into these phrases in English.

Teacher:　Who do you love?

(*Yahata repeats after her teacher.*)

20　*Narrator:*　❻ Yahata carefully practices pronunciation and intonation to

([1]) ([2]) ([3])

([4]) ([5]) ([6])

([7]).

Yahata:　❼ I want to ([1]) ([2])

25　([3]) ([4]) ([5])

([6]) ([7]) as well as I can

in Japanese. I will be happy if I can devote myself to this mission.

Narrator:　Yahata believes that if she can touch as many people around

30　the world as possible, even one or two at a time, her hard work and dedication will all be worth it.

---

❹ 核兵器は非合理で非道徳で違法 である

❺ 私も自分ができることをやる必要がある

❻ 彼女の言いたいことをできるだけ気持ちを込めて表す

❼ 英語で自分を表現することができる

Notes: (p. 34) ℓ. 1　has という発音が聞こえるが、文法的にはこのようにhave が正しい

ℓ. 8　映像ではin の直前にon という音が聞こえるが、不要

Review the Key Expressions

各問、選択肢から適切な単語を選び、英文を完成させましょう。なお、余分な単語が1語ずつあります。

1. 多くの国では、買い物客が食費に使えたはずのお金をインフレが<u>奪って</u>しまった。

   In many countries, (　　　　　　) has (＿＿＿＿＿＿) shoppers (＿＿＿＿＿＿　　)
   the (　　　　　　) they would (　　　　　) (　　　　　　) on food.

spent	of	money	inflation	deprived	with	have

2. 警察の捜査班が到着して、行方不明の女性の捜査が<u>本格的に</u>始まった。

   The (　　　　　) (　　　　　　) the (　　　　　　) woman began
   (＿＿＿＿＿) (＿＿＿＿＿＿) after the (　　　　　) (　　　　　　) arrived.

repeat	earnest	missing	search	for	squad	in	police

3. この申し込み書を、できるだけ早く提出する［送る］ことを<u>お勧めします</u>。

   You (＿＿＿＿＿＿) (＿＿＿＿＿＿) to (　　　　　) (　　　　　　) this
   (　　　　) form (　　　　) (　　　　　) as possible.

as	are	application	soon	able	encouraged	in	send

4. コロナウイルス（を取り巻く）状況のせいで、以前のようには部活に<u>集中［専念］</u>できない。

   I can't (＿＿＿＿＿＿) (＿＿＿＿＿＿) to club (　　　　　) like I (　　　　　)
   (　　　　) do, (　　　　　) of the corona virus situation.

to	used	devote	am	activities	myself	because

Discussion Questions

1. What are you doing to improve your English communication skills? Explain.

2. Would you be interested in travelling on the Peace Boat and participating in its international activities? Why?

UNIT 07

Building Playgrounds in Disaster-Hit Communities

被災地の子どもに遊び場を!

BUILDING PLAYGROUNDS IN DISASTER-HIT COMMUNITIES

特定非営利活動法人の Playground of Hope は、災害被災地や児童養護施設に遊具等を設置する事業に取り組んでいる。「遊び」は子どもの心身両面の健全な発達に不可欠なので、その環境を整備することは極めて重要である。Michael Anop さんはその法人の中心的な役目を担い、市民参加型のこの事業で遊具の設置、修理に奔走している。

放送日 2021/4/23

Words & Phrases

CD 14

以下の単語や熟語の音声を聞きながら発音に注意し、意味を確認しましょう。

☐ **disaster-hit**　　被災した
例文 The group helped people in a *disaster-hit* area of Kumamoto Prefecture.
　　そのグループは熊本県の被災地の人たちを援助した。
☐ **municipal**　　市営の
☐ to **house** [hauz]　　～に場所を与える、～を収容する
例文 The refugees are being *housed* in temporary accommodations.
　　その難民たちは臨時の避難所に住んでいる。
☐ to **compel**　　〈人・もの〉に強いる
☐ **lifespan**　　寿命
☐ to **tighten**　　～を締める
☐ **handiwork**　　手仕事
☐ to **wane**　　衰える、弱まる
☐ **undaunted**　　ひるまない
☐ **calling**　　天職

以下は、遊び、公園の遊具、テーマパークの乗り物などに関する表現です。下の枠内から適切な語彙を選び、空所に入れましょう。

- 遊具　　　　　　　　　playground (　　　　　　　　　　　1)
- ブランコ　　　　　　　(　　　　　　　　2)
- 滑り台　　　　　　　　(　　　　　　　　3)
- シーソー　　　　　　　seesaw
- 砂場　　　　　　　　　(　　　　　　　　4)
- うんてい　　　　　　　(　　　　　　　　5) bars
- かくれんぼ　　　　　　(　　　　　　　　6)
- 鬼ごっこ　　　　　　　(　　　　　　　　7)
- テーマパーク　　　　　(　　　　　　　　8) park
- ジェットコースター　　(　　　　　　　　9) coaster
- 遊園地　　　　　　　　(　　　　　　　　10) park
- 観覧車　　　　　　　　Ferris (　　　　　　　　11)
- 迷路　　　　　　　　　(　　　　　　　　12)
- お化け屋敷　　　　　　(　　　　　　　　13) house
- メリーゴーランド　　　merry-go-round
- バイキング(海賊船型大型ブランコ)　　　(　　　　　　　　14) ride

amusement	equipment	haunted	hide-and-seek	maze	monkey
pirate ship	roller	sandbox	slide	swing	wheel	tag	theme

ニュースを見て、内容と合っているものは T 、違っているものは F を選びましょう。

1. Anop was motivated to join this project because he saw the children's need.　T・F

2. Anop comes from the U.S. and has young children.　T・F

3. This playground equipment usually needs repair or replacement every 20 years.　T・F

1 ニュースをもう一度見て、各問の空所に入る適切な選択肢を a ~ c から選びましょう。

1. At first Anop thought the volunteer group would build _____ playgrounds.

    a. a small number of
    b. 60 or more
    c. around 150

2. Shiota Kenichi _____.

    a. lost his home due to a landslide
    b. contacted Anop and did maintenance work
    c. met Anop in the U.S. when he was younger

3. Anop is planning to _____.

    a. move back to his home country soon
    b. stay in Kesennuma and open a business
    c. help more children enjoy play time

2 以下の各情報を、ニュースに出てきた順序に並べましょう。

1. Anop says he and his team focus on the importance of play.

2. Anop opened a city park in Kesennuma.

3. Shiota Kenichi maintained the playground with Anop.

4. Anop has lived in the metropolitan area for 30 years.

CDの音声を聞いて、News Story の ❶～❼ の文中にある空所に適切な単語を書き入れましょう。音声は2回繰り返されます。

Narrator: The sight of children laughing, smiling, screaming in excitement. For Michael Anop, it's been a source of motivation since the March 11 disaster.

5　　　That event put his life on an unexpected path. He recently marked the opening of a **municipal** park in the city of Kesennuma. ❶ The land was (¹) (²) (³) (⁴) (⁵) (⁶), a whole community wiped out. ❷ Now, it **houses** the largest playground

10　　Anop and (¹) (²) (³) (⁴) (⁵) (⁶) (⁷), with the help *of former* residents.

❶ かつては、想像も
つかない場所だっ
た

❷ 彼のチームがその
地域に建設した

Originally from the U.S., Anop has called the Tokyo area

15　　home for 30 years. He started traveling to the northeast as a volunteer in 2011, delivering foods to people in temporary housing. That's when he noticed there were few parks or playgrounds. Being a parent with young children himself, he felt **compelled** to change that.

20　　❸ (¹) (²) (³) (⁴) (⁵) (⁶) (⁷) and recruited the team of volunteers. At first he thought they would only put up a handful, but he soon realized demand was high, and set up a non-profit

25　　group. To date, they've built more than 60 playgrounds. They also make sure the structures stay in good shape. Their average **lifespan** is ten years, so Anop expected this one, which dates back to 2012, would need major work when he came to do repairs.

❸ 彼は資材購入のた
めにスポンサーを
見つけた

30　**Anop:** Usually these are all loose, and they need to be **tightened**.

　　Woman: Really?

Anop: Yeah, it's crazy.

Narrator: That means the community has been taking good care of it all these years, a pleasant surprise for Anop.

5　One of the people who's been maintaining the playground is Shiota Kenichi. He lost his home and his business to the tsunami. As he worked to rebuild, he realized his children needed a place to play. So, he contacted Anop's team. ❹ Their **handiwork** (　　　　 ¹) (　　　　 ²) (　　　　 ³) (　　　　 ⁴), (　　　　 ⁵)

10　(　　　　 ⁶) and even grandparents in the area.

❹ 子供たちとその親たちをひきつけていた

Local families gathered in early April to help with the maintenance work. ❺ They included Shiota and his son, who (　　　　 ¹) (　　　　 ²) (　　　　 ³) (　　　　 ⁴) (　　　　 ⁵) (　　　　 ⁶).

❺ その建造物で遊んで育った

15　**Narrator:** ❻ Anop says (　　　　 ¹) (　　　　 ²) (　　　　 ³) (　　　　 ⁴) (　　　　 ⁵) (　　　　 ⁶). Fundraising is getting harder as interest in the recovery effort **wanes**, and because of the pandemic, but he's **undaunted**.

❻ これからの道のりには困難がないわけではない

20　**Michael Anop** *(Representative Director, Playground of Hope):* We're the only one focusing on the power of play, so if we don't do it, who will? ❼ There is (　　　　 ¹) (　　　　 ²) (　　　　 ³) (　　　　 ⁴) (　　　　 ⁵) (　　　　 ⁶) (　　　　 ⁷), and so many other children that need

25　our support.

❼ まだやることがたくさんある

Narrator: Anop says this is his **calling**, to provide an outlet for children in stressful situations, not only in the northeast, but across Japan. And he is determined to keep going as long as he is in a position to help. Yotsumoto Jun, NHK World.

Notes:（p. 40）ℓ. 12　映像ではこの of は from で代用されているが、of のほうがしぜん

　　　　　ℓ. 13　formal のように聞こえるが、former が正しい

Review the Key Expressions

各問、選択肢から適切な単語を選び、英文を完成させましょう。なお、余分な単語が1語ずつあります。

1. きょう、みずきに会ったとき、最初彼女は怒ったような顔に見えたけど、体調が悪かったことを後で知った。

   When I saw Mizuki today, (＿＿＿＿＿＿) (＿＿＿＿＿＿) she (＿＿＿＿＿)
   angry, but (＿＿＿＿) I (＿＿＿＿＿) she was (＿＿＿＿＿).

   | sick   first   at   cold   later   looked   realized |

2. 私は一日おきにジョギングし、時々体育施設で運動をしているので、体調がいい。

   I (＿＿＿＿＿) every (＿＿＿＿＿) day and often (＿＿＿＿＿)
   (＿＿＿＿＿) at the (＿＿＿＿＿), so I'm in (＿＿＿＿＿) (＿＿＿＿＿).

   | other   work   gym   shape   out   good   jog   grade |

3. 美香は動物が好きで、いつもよく自分の猫や犬を世話する。

   Mika (＿＿＿＿＿) (＿＿＿＿＿), and she always (＿＿＿＿＿＿)
   (＿＿＿＿＿) (＿＿＿＿＿＿) (＿＿＿＿＿＿) her cats and dogs.

   | loves   of   care   takes   with   good   animals |

4. 給与さえ良ければ [〜である限り]、私はどこであってもパートで働くつもりがあります。

   As (＿＿＿＿＿＿) (＿＿＿＿＿) the (＿＿＿＿＿) is good, I'm (＿＿＿＿＿)
   (＿＿＿＿＿) work (＿＿＿＿＿) part-time.

   | long   willing   few   as   anyplace   pay   to |

Discussion Questions

1. What kind of volunteer work have you done or would you like to do? Why?

2. What are your favorite rides at big amusement parks or at theme parks?

42

UNIT 08

Climate Change Activist Comes of Age

高校生、COP での気づき

LIMATE CHANGE ACTIVIST COMES OF AGE

気候変動に対する国際的な取り組みが進む中、グラスゴーにおいてCOP 26が開催され、脱化石燃料の動きを後押しする重要な一歩を踏み出した。世界の環境保護活動家が会場近くで集会を開いて、各国の惨状を示し地球温暖化に対する緊急な対策を訴えた。日本からも高校生たちが参加し、今後日本のとるべき道を熱く主張した。

放送日 2021/12/2

Words & Phrases

○ CD 16

以下の単語や熟語の音声を聞きながら発音に注意し、意味を確認しましょう。

- [ ] **activist** 活動家
- [ ] to **come of age** 成熟期に達する
  - 例文 Renewable energy has *come of age*.
    再生可能エネルギーの使用が十分発達した。
- [ ] **taste** 経験
  - 例文 Miho got a *taste* of volunteer work during the summer.
    美穂は夏の間ボランティアを経験した。
- [ ] **green** 環境保護の
- [ ] **commitment** 公約、約束
- [ ] **coal-fired** 石炭火力の
- [ ] to **emit** 〈熱、光など〉を出す、放つ
- [ ] **carbon dioxide** 二酸化炭素
- [ ] to **account for** ～の割合を占める
- [ ] to **sting** 傷つける
- [ ] **second thoughts** 考え直すこと、再考
- [ ] **solidarity** 連帯、共有
- [ ] **vital** 生死に関わる

以下は、環境問題に関する表現です。下の枠内から適切な単語を選び、空所に入れましょう。

1. レジ袋を再利用することは、環境への悪影響を減らす手軽な方法だ。
   Reusing plastic bags is an easy way to reduce your (　　　　　　　) (　　　　　　　).

2. 温室効果ガスの排出を削減するため、人々は公共交通機関を使うべきだ。
   People should use (　　　　　　　) transportation to reduce (　　　　　　) gas
   (　　　　　　).

3. 再生可能エネルギーには太陽光や風力、水力、地熱などがある。
   (　　　　　　　) energy sources include (　　　　　　　) , (　　　　　　　) , water and
   geothermal heat.

4. 私たちは未来の人々のために、持続可能な生活スタイルを取り入れなければならない。
   We must adopt a (　　　　　　　) lifestyle for future generations.

5. 光熱費を減らすために節電している。
   I'm (　　　　　　) on (　　　　　　　) to reduce my heating and lighting expenses.

6. 環境に優しい生活を始めることは必ずしも簡単ではない。
   It isn't always easy to start (　　　　　　) (　　　　　　　).

7. レストランでは割り箸 [使い捨ての箸] を普通のものに替えるのはいい考えですか。
   Is it a good idea for restaurants to replace (　　　　　　　) chopsticks with reusable
   ones?

electricity	emissions	environmental	footprint	going
green	greenhouse	public	renewable	saving
single-use	solar	sustainable	wind	

ニュースを見て、内容と合っているものは T、違っているものは F を選びましょう。

1. In Japan, people rely on coal for less than a quarter of their energy supply. T・F

2. Yuho, who joined the rally in Glasgow, was criticized on social media. T・F

3. Yuho's confidence as an activist returned after she saw the protesters' unity at the
   rally. T・F

1 ニュースをもう一度見て、各問の空所に入る適切な選択肢を a～c から選びましょう。

1. Yuho belongs to _____.

    a. an international traveling circle
    b. a green group in Japan
    c. the science club at a senior high school

2. Yuho started her work fighting against climate change after she _____.

    a. heard about the ice that is thawing in Greenland
    b. arrived at Glasgow to join the rally among green activists
    c. discovered that a coal-fueled plant would be built near her hometown

3. At the COP 26 conference, members aimed to limit the average global increases in temperature to _____.

    a. 0.5 degrees Celsius
    b. 1.5 degrees Centigrade
    c. 2.5 degrees Fahrenheit

2 以下の各情報を、ニュースに出てきた順序に並べましょう。

1. Sweden's Greta Thunberg is among the protesters at the rally in Glasgow.

2. During the conference, an agreement was reached about limiting temperature increases.

3. Yuna is a high school student who belongs to a Japanese environmental group.

4. An activist is making a speech claiming her people have water shortages.

CD 17

CDの音声を聞いて、News Story の ❶〜❼ の文中にある空所に適切な単語を書き入れましょう。音声は2回繰り返されます。

Anchor: ❶ World leaders who took part in last month's U.N. climate change conference were under pressure (¹) (²) (³) (⁴) (⁵) (⁶) (⁷).

❶ 環境を守るために もっと行う

5   One of those demanding stronger measures was a high school student from Japan. Our next story looks at her first **taste** of campaigning on the global stage.

Narrator: Some of the protestors in Glasgow were old hands in **green** activism, including Sweden's Greta Thunberg.

10 *Greta Thunberg:* Change is not going to come from inside there. That is not leadership. (*Pointing at the group in front of her*) This is leadership....

Narrator: Others were new comers. High school student Hara Yuho belongs to a Japanese environmental group set up in 2019.

15 *Hara Yuho (Fridays For Future Japan):* We may be the first Japanese high school student activists to participate in the event, so I hope to make friends with people from all over the world and tell them about the current situation in Japan.

Narrator: Yuho's **commitment** to fighting climate change started after
20   hearing about plans to build a new **coal-fired** power plant near her hometown.

Hara: (*Using a microphone*) Coal **emits** more **carbon dioxide** than any other energy source!

Narrator: Despite the protests, work to build the coal plant is going
25   ahead. Yuho needed new ideas. ❷ COP 26 seemed the ideal place to (¹) (²) (³) (⁴) (⁵) (⁶). ❸ (¹) (²) (³) (⁴) (⁵)
30   (⁶) (⁷). Yuho and her fellow students arrived in Glasgow at the end of October.

❷ 気候変動への活動 についてもっと知 るようになる

❸ 彼女の両親や学校 も支持をした

Narrator: The group is demanding a ban on coal-fired power production. Coal **accounts for** about 30 percent of Japan's energy supply.

Protesters: No coal Japan!

Narrator: But they're not the only ones fired up. On social media, the students come under attack.

Narrator: The criticism **stings**. Was she qualified to be an activist? Yuho was having **second thoughts**.

❹ (¹) (²) (³)
(⁴) (⁵) (⁶)
(⁷). So *were* the *action*[s] on the streets.

❺ (¹) (²) (³)
(⁴) (⁵) (⁶)
(⁷). This is a first for Yuho, both in the scale of the protest and the passion of those taking part.

Protester 1: (*Giving a speech*) I *grew up* seeing people around me walk long distances because their water sources are dried up.

Protester 2: In Latin America we are already suffering the consequences of the climate crisis from fire to historic *floods*.

Narrator: The speakers offered inspiration and **solidarity**. Yuho's confidence is returning.

Hara: ❻ I realized that climate change is very much
(¹) (²) (³)
(⁴) (⁵) (⁶)
(⁷). I'm glad that I came here because I'm more certain of what I want to do and what I should focus on.

Narrator: In the end, the negotiators agreed on a commitment for limiting increases in global average temperature to 1.5 degrees Celsius. ❼ Yuho (¹) (²)
(³) (⁴) (⁵)
(⁶) on this **vital** global issue.

❹ 会議での交渉は熱を帯びた

❺ 何千人ものデモ参加者が市街を埋めた

❻ （〜は）貧困や民族の問題と結びついている

❼ （〜について）声を出し続けるつもりだ

Notes: （p. 47）ℓ. 10　were は発音が明瞭ではないが、語彙的にはこれが考えられうる

ℓ. 10　action は聞きとりにくいが文法的には -s が必要

ℓ. 15　grew up は訛りがある発音

ℓ. 18　floods は発音に誤りがあると考えられる

各問、選択肢から適切な単語を選び、英文を完成させましょう。なお、余分な単語が1語ずつあります。

1. デザインの改良のおかげで、最近の10年間でLEDは十分発達した。

   LEDs have (＿＿＿＿＿＿＿) (＿＿＿＿＿＿＿) (＿＿＿＿＿＿＿) in the (＿＿＿＿＿＿＿)
   ten years (＿＿＿＿＿) (＿＿＿＿＿) (＿＿＿＿＿) in their design.

   | thanks | of | last | come | age | improvements | next | to |

2. 留学生の数が増加していて、今ではこの大学の学生数の8パーセントを占める。

   The (＿＿＿＿＿) of (＿＿＿＿＿) students is (＿＿＿＿＿) and now
   (＿＿＿＿＿＿＿) (＿＿＿＿＿＿＿) eight percent of this college's (＿＿＿＿＿).

   | in | for | number | international | enrollment | accounts | increasing |

3. 最近は航空運賃が値上がりしているので、この夏パリに行くかどうか決めかねている。

   Given the (＿＿＿＿＿) (＿＿＿＿＿＿＿) in airfare prices, I'm (＿＿＿＿＿)
   (＿＿＿＿＿＿＿) (＿＿＿＿＿＿) about (＿＿＿＿＿＿＿) to Paris this summer.

   | increase | thoughts | recent | second | decrease | having | flying |

4. 長い話し合いの末、両者がお互いに譲歩しあうことで、最終的に話がまとまった。

   (＿＿＿＿＿＿＿) the (＿＿＿＿＿＿＿), both parties (＿＿＿＿＿) and agreed to
   (＿＿＿＿＿) (＿＿＿＿＿) after a long (＿＿＿＿＿).

   | discussion | end | meet | compromised | all | in | halfway |

1. What environmentally friendly things do you do? Why? If nothing, why not?

2. What do you think of senior high school students participating in international rallies? Explain.

UNIT 09

Tech for Pets Takes Off

ペットテック

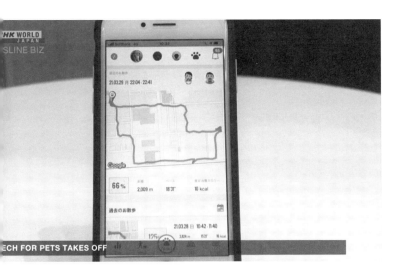

犬や猫などのペットは私たち家族の一員という意識が年々高まっている。ペット用品の展示会を見ても、基本的なケアやおしゃれはもちろん、健康食品やサプリメント、最先端技術を駆使した生活・健康管理グッズに人気が集まる。今日のリポートでは、最新の情報から人気のペットケア商品をいくつか紹介する。

放送日 2021/6/23

Words & Phrases

CD 18

以下の単語や熟語の音声を聞きながら発音に注意し、意味を確認しましょう。

☐ to **take off**　　　（急に）人気が出る
☐ to **fuel**　　　　　～を奨励する、あおる
☐ **cutting-edge**　　最先端の
　例文 The new smartphone features *cutting-edge* technology.
　　　新しいスマホは最先端技術を特徴としている。
☐ **furry**　　　　　　柔毛で覆われた
☐ to **keep tabs on**　～を見張る、～に気をつける
☐ **tracker**　　　　　追跡するもの
☐ **chubby**　　　　　〈特に子どもについて〉丸々と太った、ぽっちゃりした
　例文 The little baby was pink and *chubby*.
　　　その小さい赤ちゃんは健康的でぽっちゃりした感じだった。
☐ **feline**　　　　　　猫の
☐ to **crunch**　　　　〈大量のデータ〉を高速処理する
☐ **errand**　　　　　用事
☐ **grooming**　　　　毛づくろい
☐ **start-up**　　　　　新興企業

以下は、ペットに関する表現です。下の枠内から適切な単語を選び、空所に入れましょう。

1. ペットを何か飼っていますか。　Do you (　　　　　　) any pets?

2. 誕生日プレゼントとして、父が亀を買ってくれました。

   My father got me a (　　　　　　) for my birthday.

3. 私はタマという名前のぶち猫を飼っています。　I have a tabby cat (　　　　　　) Tama.

4. どんな犬〔猫〕ですか。　What's your dog〔cat〕like?

   a. オスの子犬で遊び好きです。　He's a (　　　　　　) and very (　　　　　　).

   b. 年のいったメス猫ですが、頭が良く、愛情にあふれています。

      She is an older cat, but still very (　　　　　　) and (　　　　　　).

   c. 彼女は子猫です。いたずらばかりしますが、抱っこしたくなります。

      She is a (　　　　　　). She is sometimes (　　　　　　), but very

      (　　　　　　).

5. 毎日、夕方に犬の散歩に行きます。　I (　　　　　　) my dog every evening.

6. 私たちの分譲マンションでは、ペットは許可されていません。

   We're not (　　　　　　) to have pets in our (　　　　　　).

7. 私は猫派です。犬は吠えるので好きではありません。

   I am a (　　　　　　). I don't like dogs because they bark a lot.

8. 私には喘息があります。猫が発作を誘発するかもしれません。

   I have (　　　　　　). Cats may (　　　　　　) attacks.

affectionate	allowed	asthma	called	cat person
condo	cuddly	have	intelligent	kitten	naughty	playful
	puppy	trigger	turtle	walk	

ニュースを見て、内容と合っているものは T 、違っているものは F を選びましょう。

1. This pet boom has little to do with the COVID-19 pandemic.　　　T・F

2. The camera is designed to catch your pet's movements at home.　　T・F

3. The start-up seen in this report is studying the activities of less than 700 cats.

   　　　　　　　　　　　　　　　　　　　　　　　　　　　　　　T・F

1 ニュースをもう一度見て、各問の空所に入る適切な選択肢を a ~ c から選びましょう。

1. The tag a man shows provides information about _____.

   a. the weather for the day
   b. an animal's mood
   c. calories used by a dog

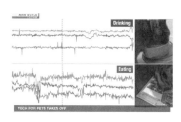

2. According to the graph, the top lines with short wavelengths show that the _____.

   a. cat's movements are small
   b. cat is eating food
   c. cat's stress level is very high

3. According to the CEO of high-tech products for pet cats, _____.

   a. there are billions of pet cats worldwide
   b. pet cats around the world act similarly
   c. the pet tech business was more popular in the past

2 以下はニュースの概要です。空所に適切な単語を書き入れましょう。語頭の文字（群）は与えてあります。

Cat and dog owners are now more interested in high-tech devices for taking care of their pets. A trade show introduced ingenious products using (**cut** [1]) technologies, such as a (**c** [2]) which follows pets' movements and a tag which functions like a (**fit** [3]) tracker. A big hit is a system in which cats' movements are shown and converted into lines on a (**gr** [4]). Those lines can tell what pets are doing. The owners also may learn what care their pets need. Pet tech is a new (**in** [5]) and may become a big future business.

Listen to the News Story

CDの音声を聞いて、News Story の ❶〜❼ の文中にある空所に適切な単語を書き入れましょう。音声は２回繰り返されます。

Anchor: The coronavirus pandemic has **fueled** a boom in pet adoptions around the world as people spend more time at home. Cat and dog owners in Japan are getting help from **cutting-edge** technologies that let them know what their furry friends may want or need.

Narrator: ❶ At a trade show held recently in Tokyo, a company demonstrates a camera that lets people **keep tabs on** their pets (¹) (²) (³) (⁴) (⁵) (⁶). The camera follows the dog or cat while it moves.

❶ 彼らが外出している間に

This tag is a fitness **tracker** for your dog. Using GPS, it shows how far the dog has walked and calculates the calories burned.

Tamura Toshiki (CEO, Pontely): Dogs shouldn't get **chubby**. ❷ This tool (¹) (²) (³) (⁴) (⁵) (⁶).

❷ 体重管理のお手伝いをする

Narrator: ❸ A big seller is this system that can give people a minute by minute (¹) (²) (³) (⁴) (⁵) (⁶) (⁷). A censor in the collar tracks **feline** movements and other daily activities. It then converts the information into data lines shown on a graph.

❸ 猫が何をやっているかを説明すること

The top lines with short wavelengths indicate small movements. Translation: the cat is drinking water. The graph below with longer wavelengths shows big movements, meaning the cat is eating food. ❹ AI **crunches** the data and records it in an activity log that owners can check when (¹) (²) (³) (⁴) (⁵) (⁶) (⁷) or out running **errands**.

❹ 彼らが職場で休憩している

❺ This cat (¹) (²)
(³) (⁴) (⁵)
(⁶). The system also notifies the owner of
unusual behavior. Increased **grooming** can be indicative
of higher stress levels. ❻ Exercise decreasing over
several days may tell the owner it's (¹)
(²) (³) (⁴)
(⁵) (⁶) (⁷).

This is the **start-up** that developed this device. Eighteen
months after launching, it's tracking the activity of about
7,000 cats. ❼ The company says the accuracy of its daily
activity analysis is improving as (¹)
(²) (³) (⁴)
(⁵) (⁶) (⁷).

The CEO sees great potential for growth, given that feline
behavior is universal.

Iyo Yukiko (CEO, Rabo): There are 600 million pet cats around the world, and
they act similarly, so I want to expand globally as quickly as
possible.

Narrator: Pet tech is a new industry that is just starting to take off in
Japan.

❺ ちょうど予定通りに昼
ご飯を食べていた

❻ 彼らの猫の体調を調べ
る（べき）ときである

❼ 人工知能がこれらの猫
からより多くのデータ
を集める

各問、選択肢から適切な単語を選び、英文を完成させましょう。なお、余分な単語が1語
ずつあります。

1. その新しい掃除機はリモコンで操作されるので、急に人気が出た。

   The new (　　　　　) cleaner (＿＿＿＿＿)(＿＿＿＿＿) because

   (　　　)(　　　　　) be (　　　　) by (　　　　　) control.

remote	it	vacuum	off	can	down	operated	took

2. その医師は、定期的に健康診断を受けて健康に気をつけるように私に勧めた。

   The doctor (　　　　　) that I (＿＿＿＿＿)(＿＿＿＿＿) on my

   (　　　　　) by (　　　　　) regular (　　　　　)(　　　　　).

off	check-ups	tabs	recommended	health	keep	medical	getting

3. 私たちは3時間続けて仕事をしています。15分休憩してコーヒーでも飲みましょう。

   We've (　　　　)(　　　　　) three (　　　　) hours. Let's

   (＿＿＿＿) a (　　　　　)(＿＿＿＿＿) for 15 minutes.

coffee	been	take	drink	straight	working	break

4. お客様の苦情にできるだけすばやく、確実に対処してください。

   (　　　　)(　　　　　) that you (　　　　)(　　　　　　) customer

   complaints as (＿＿＿＿＿)(　　　　　)(＿＿＿＿＿).

with	make	as	sure	such	possible	deal	quickly

1. If you decide to get a pet, what kind will it be: a dog, cat or some other animal? Why?

2. Name one thing that you are willing to spend your money on. Explain why.

Hairdressers Given a Shot at Independence

モール型のヘアサロン

AIRDRESSERS GIVEN A SHOT AT INDEPENDENCE

初期費用なし、定額家賃だけでオーナーになれる「モール型サロン」。その設立の背景にはある理念がある。経営上のリスクを冒さずに自分のサロンが持てるように美容師たちを支援することである。こうした個室型サロンが開業できる独立開業支援サービスは、将来の真の独立を目標にする有能な美容師にとって大きな追い風となる。

放送日 2021/12/2

Words & Phrases

◎ CD 20

以下の単語や熟語の音声を聞きながら発音に注意し、意味を確認しましょう。

- □ to **give** 〈someone〉 **a shot at**　　人に〜の機会を与える
- □ **path**　　　　　　　道、通り道
- □ to **lay out**　　　　〜を設計する、レイアウトする
- □ **qualified**　　　　　資格のある、免許を有する
- □ **posh**　　　　　　　高級な、おしゃれな
- □ to **subdivide**　　　〜を再分割する、細分する
- □ to **launch**　　　　　〜を立ち上げる、設立する

例文 The government should *launch* an investigation into the plane crash.
　　政府はその旅客機墜落の捜査を始めるべきだ。

- □ **regular client**　　　得意客、顧客
- □ **security deposit**　　敷金、保証金
- □ to **envision**　　　　〈未来のことなど〉を思い描く、想像する

例文 This outcome was not at all what I had *envisioned*.
　　この結果は、私が思い描いていたものと全然違っていた。

以下は、美容院などに関する記述です。下の枠内から適切な単語を選び、空所に入れましょう。

1. リサは、美容師に新しくパーマをかけてもらった。
   Lisa got a (　　　　　　) (　　　　　　) from her (　　　　　　).

2. 髪がちょっと伸びてきたので、美容師に調髪の予約をした。
   My hair is getting a (　　　　　　) long, so I have (　　　　　　) an
   (　　　　　　) with my hairdresser for a trim.

3. 母の髪は手入れがとても簡単なので、美容院にはめったに行かない。
   My mother's hair is very (　　　　　　) to (　　　　　　), so she (　　　　　　)
   goes to the beauty (　　　　　　).

4. 明日の午後、新しい床屋で散髪してもらうつもりだ。
   I'm going to (　　　　　　) a (　　　　　　) at a new barber's tomorrow
   afternoon.

5. コズメトロジストは、髪だけではなくマニキュア、ペディキュアそれにメイクもやってくれる。
   A cosmetologist not only works with hair, but can also (　　　　　　) manicures,
   (　　　　　　) and (　　　　　　).

6. あの床屋で髪をめちゃくちゃにされた。もう行かない。
   That barber (　　　　　　) my hair. I don't go to him (　　　　　　).

7. うちの高校ではツーブロックヘアスタイルは認められていない。
   At my senior high school, students are (　　　　　　) (　　　　　　) to get
   (　　　　　　) hairstyles.

8. 小さい頃、僕はマッシュヘアだった。　I had a (　　　　　　) when I was young.

anymore	appointment	bit	bowl cut	do	easy	fix	
get	haircut	hairstylist	made	makeup	new	not	parlor
pedicures	perm	permitted	rarely	ruined	undercut		

1st Viewing ≫ **Watch the News**

ニュースを見て、内容と合っているものはＴ、違っているものはＦを選びましょう。

1. Shimizu is a hairdresser and the president of a leasing company.　T・F

2. There are approximately 50,000 hairdressers in Japan.　T・F

3. Shimizu says that it's easier now for hairdressers to rent spaces cheaply.　T・F

>> **Understand the News**

1 ニュースをもう一度見て、各問の空所に入る適切な選択肢を a ~ c から選びましょう。

1. Shimizu opened _____.

   a. beauty salons at two locations in Minami-Aoyama
   b. four facilities in Tokyo for renting spaces
   c. his main office in Ginza

2. Shimizu thought up the idea of subdividing large floor spaces for _____.

   a. business representatives of various companies
   b. any staff members to use as a shared satellite office
   c. tenants starting work as hairstylists

3. Kojima decided to _____.

   a. keep his job as a hired stylist
   b. use Shimizu's renting service
   c. open a hair salon by himself

2 ニュースに関して、空所に入る適切な数字を枠内から選びましょう（余分な選択肢があります）。

1. There are (   ) beauty parlors on two floors of this building in Tokyo's Minami-Aoyama District.

2. These two young hairdressers had (   ) regular customers at a leading beauty parlor.

3. Setting up a hair salon may cost over (   ) dollars.

4. The minimum monthly rent charged by Shimizu is over (   ) dollars.

18	19	20	50	150	500	1,200
	2,000	8,500	85,000	185,000		

CDの音声を聞いて、News Story の ❶～❼ の文中にある空所に適切な単語を書き入れましょう。音声は2回繰り返されます。

Anchor: ❶ The coronavirus pandemic is creating (　　　　 1)
(　　　　 2) (　　　　 3) (　　　　 4)
(　　　　 5) (　　　　 6) (　　　　 7).
A venture has been making use of these spaces to put
5 hairdressers on a **path** to independence.

Narrator: This hair salon is in Tokyo's trendy and high-priced Minami-Aoyama District. It has a floor space of about 15 square meters. Walking out of the salon, there are 19 beauty parlors on two floors. It's **laid out** like a shopping mall. It's been open
10 since June. Shimizu Hidehito is a **qualified** hairdresser and president of the company that leases these spaces. In the past two years, he has opened similar facilities in four locations in Tokyo, including two in the **posh** Ginza District.

❷ Owners of commercial buildings (　　　　 1)
15 (　　　　 2) (　　　　 3) (　　　　 4)
(　　　　 5) (　　　　 6) (　　　　 7).
❸ Restaurants are closing, and (　　　　 1)
(　　　　 2) (　　　　 3) (　　　　 4)
(　　　　 5) (　　　　 6). Building owners
20 looking for tenants sign leases with Shimizu, often at
discounted rents.

There are more than 500,000 hairdressers in Japan. Many
dream of opening a salon of their own in central Tokyo, where
there is growing demand for their services. So, Shimizu
25 came up with the idea of renting large floors, **subdividing**
them, and letting others use the spaces. ❹ The idea is to
give his tenants (　　　　 1) (　　　　 2)
(　　　　 3) (　　　　 4) (　　　　 5)
(　　　　 6) (　　　　 7).

30 *Shimizu Hidehito (CEO, Salons Japan):* Since rents are becoming cheaper, it's easier for us to provide hairdressers with great locations for reasonable prices.

❶ 職場の空室数の増加

❷ 世界的感染の広がりの間にテナントの 数が減少している

❸ 在宅勤務している人が増えている

❹ 自分の事業を始める機会

58

Narrator: These two young hairdressers used Shimizu's service as a way of jointly **launching** their own business. They used to have about 500 **regular clients** when they worked at a major beauty parlor, but they felt uncertain about their future.

5　***Kojima Yoshiaki*** *(Hairdresser):* I wasn't sure if I should keep working as a hired stylist, but I wasn't ready to take the risk of opening a salon by myself. ❺ The service (　　　　　　¹)

　　　　(　　　　²) (　　　　³) (　　　　⁴)

　　　　(　　　　⁵) (　　　　⁶).

❺ （～が）自分の店を開くのを助けてくれた

10　**Narrator:** Launching a hair salon can cost more than 85,000 dollars. That includes equipment and interior design. Salons in Shimizu's spaces include basic features like shampoo bowls. The minimum monthly rent is around 2,300 dollars. Tenants pay a **security deposit** equal to three months' rent. Many

15　say they are now earning three times as much as when they were employees.

Hasegawa Shun *(Hairdresser):* ❻ My next goal is to (　　　　¹)

　　　　(　　　　²) (　　　　³) (　　　　⁴)

　　　　(　　　　⁵) (　　　　⁶) (　　　　⁷).

❻ 貯金してもっと大きな店を開く（こと）

20　**Shimizu:** The business model I **envision** is that they work here for two to three years to develop business skills and then open their own salons.

Narrator: Shimizu hopes the hairdressers will learn business know-how, such as price-setting and profit management, which

25　will help them with their next step. ❼ He is planning to

　　　　(　　　　¹) (　　　　²) (　　　　³)

　　　　(　　　　⁴) (　　　　⁵) (　　　　⁶).

❼ 全国に営業を展開させる

各問、選択肢から適切な単語を選び、英文を完成させましょう。なお、余分な単語が１語
ずつあります。

1. 私はよく、バスに乗っている時間を、スマホで英字新聞を読むのにあてて［活用して］いる。

I often (　　　　　　) (　　　　　　) (　　　　　　) the time I (　　　　　)
(　　　　　) the bus by (　　　　　) (　　　　　) newspapers on my
smartphone.

| use | with | on | spend | reading | English | make | of |

2. この作家の作品が、皆さんが随筆を書く時の（書き方の）手本になるように願っています。

I hope this writer's (　　　　　) (　　　　　) you (　　　　　) a
(　　　　　) of (　　　　　) (　　　　　) write your own essay.

| how | with | work | provides | to | much | model |

3. 私の祖父はよく、車を運転していたが、事故を起こすのが怖くて車の免許証を返納した。

My grandfather (　　　　　) (　　　　　) drive a (　　　　　), but he
(　　　　　) (　　　　　) his driver's license because he is (　　　　　) of
(　　　　　) traffic accidents.

| afraid | up | used | lot | gave | causing | due | to |

4. 新しい事業が成功したおかげで、彼は今、以前の５倍（多く）の売り上げがある。

(　　　　　) (　　　　　) the (　　　　　) of his new business, he now
(　　　　　) five (　　　　　) as (　　　　　) as he (　　　　　) to.

| success | to | times | long | much | thanks | used | makes |

1. If you were a young hairdresser, would you be interested in renting a space like this? Why?

2. How do you like to wear your hair, long or short? Do you also dye your hair? Why?

UNIT 11

Japanese Tradition Reinvented to Help Global Farming

土俵の技術でアフリカを支援

青森県立名久井農業高校が、ストックホルム青少年水大賞・国際大会でグランプリを受賞した。夏開催のこの水大賞は「水のノーベル賞」と位置付けられている。当校の発表テーマは、日本古来の土壌固化技術「たたき」を利用した土壌流出の制御と食料生産の増加で、この研究が世界大会で高く評価された。

放送日 2021/1/20

Words & Phrases

◎ CD 22

以下の単語や熟語の音声を聞きながら発音に注意し、意味を確認しましょう。

- □ to **refer to** A **as** B　A を B と呼ぶ
- □ to **submit**　　　　　～を提出する

　例文 Mike *submitted* his paper to the teacher.
　　　マイクは先生に論文を提出した。

- □ **arid**　　　　　　〈土地が〉乾燥した
- □ **pit**　　　　　　くぼみ、穴
- □ to **soil**　　　　　～を汚す
- □ **leakage**　　　　漏れ、漏水
- □ to **apply** A **to** B　A を B に応用する
- □ **lime**　　　　　　石灰
- □ to **pound**　　　　何度も強くたたく

　例文 The police *pounded* on the door to check if anyone was inside.
　　　警察は中に誰かいないか確認するため、ドアをドンドンとたたいた。

- □ **fertilizer**　　　　化学肥料
- □ **nutrient**　　　　栄養、養分
- □ to **quadruple**　　～を 4 倍にする〈cf. quad- 4, -ple 倍〉

以下は、農業に関する語彙です。空所に適切な文字を入れ、下のクロスワードを完成させましょう。

ACROSS

1. 農作物 （**p** _ _ _ _ _ _）　　　　2. 土壌 （**s** _ _ _）

3. 有機農業 （**o** _ _ _ _ _ _） farming　　4. 畜産農家 （**l i** _ _ _ _ _ _ _） farmer

5. 酪農場 （**d a** _ _ _） farm　　6. 〈穀類・野菜・果物などの〉作物 （**c** _ _ _）

7. 穀物 （**g** _ **a** _ _）　　　　8. 温室 （**g** _ _ _ _ _ _ _ _）

DOWN

1. 養鶏農家 （**p o** _ **l** _ _ _） farmer　　9. 稲作農家 （_ **i** _ _） farmer

10. ぶどうの果樹園 （_ _ _ _ **y a** _ _）　　11. りんごの果樹園　apple （_ _ _ **h a** _ _）

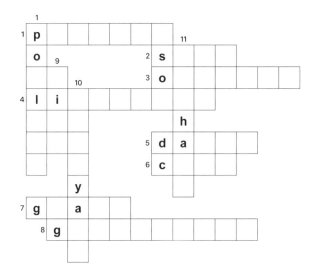

1st Viewing ≫ **Watch the News**

ニュースを見て、内容と合っているものは T 、違っているものは F を選びましょう。

1. Japanese students won the prize for international water-related research.　T・F

2. *Zai* is a farming technique in which farmers dig pits to catch water.　T・F

3. Using the *tataki* technique along with cement is still common in Japanese farming.

　T・F

1 ニュースをもう一度見て、各問の空所に入る適切な選択肢を a ~ c から選びましょう。

1. _____ sent in ideas on how to solve African water shortage problems.

   a. Twenty-nine prefectures across Japan
   b. Close to 30 countries around the world
   c. Senior high schools in Stockholm

2. To solve the water leakage problem, Miyaki _____.

   a. telephoned his grandmother in his hometown
   b. came up with a technique used in making *doma*.
   c. realized that cement should be used

3. To help the crops grow better, Miyaki's team _____.

   a. added fertilizer to the soil and hardened the mixture
   b. used lime without water and pounded the ground hard
   c. did not mix any nutrients into the solidified soil

2 右の文字列を並べ替えて単語を作り、各文の空所に入れて意味がとおるようにしましょう。語頭の文字（群）は与えてあります。

1. Japanese students received the "Nobel Prize" for water-related (**re**   ).

   [echasr]

2. The team's idea can prevent (**le**   ) of water from pits called *zai*.

   [agake]

3. *Tataki* is a traditional Japanese (**te**   ) for making *doma*.

   [quinech]

4. Miyaki's team wrote an English (**m**   ) about *tataki* and distributed it for free.

   [alaun]

CDの音声を聞いて、News Story の ❶〜❼ の文中にある空所に適切な単語を書き入れましょう。音声は2回繰り返されます。

Anchor: The Stockholm Water Prize is often **referred to as** the Nobel Prize for water-related research. In August, 2020, a group of Japanese high school students were awarded the prize for junior researchers. They developed a method using a traditional Japanese technique to help African farmers facing water shortages.

(*Students are watching the online ceremony of the 2020 Stockholm Junior Water Prize.*)

Woman: The winners are Japan.

Narrator: Students from 29 countries **submitted** solutions to major water challenges. ❶ The winner was a (¹) (²) (³) (⁴) (⁵) (⁶) (⁷) in northern Japan's Aomori Prefecture. The team's idea helped improve a traditional farming method used in many **arid** regions in Africa.

❶ 農業を勉強する高校生のチーム

Zai is a technique in which **pits** are dug in the **soil** during the rainy season to capture water. ❷ This helps corn and other crops planted in the pits (¹) (²) (³) (⁴) (⁵) (⁶). The problem with *zai* was that heavy rain could cause the soil to collapse and the stored water to leak.

❷ 乾季の間に生き残るために

One of the Japanese team members, Miyaki Takuma, learned about *zai* in class. ❸ He began (¹) (²) (³) (⁴) (⁵) (⁶) (⁷) by preventing **leakage**. He remembered the *doma* in his grandmother's home. ❹ This is the dirt floor area in a traditional Japanese house, used for (¹) (²) (³) (⁴) (⁵) (⁶) (⁷).

❸ それを改善する方法について考えること

❹ 家の中の飾り物を汚してしまうかもしれない仕事

Miyaki Takuma *(Aomori Prefectural Nakui Agricultural High School):* I learned that *doma* are made of soil using a technique called *tataki*. I **applied** the technique **to** our project.

Narrator: Soil made with this solidification technique was common in Japan before cement became available. Sumo rings are also made using *tataki*. Soil becomes more water-resistant when it is mixed with water and **lime**, then hardened by **pounding**.

It occurred to Miyaki and his team that *tataki* could solve *zai*'s leakage issue. They started to experiment. They tried numerous times to come up with a way to prevent water leakage using the *tataki* method. They also mixed **fertilizer** into the solidified soil, thinking the **nutrients** would dissolve in the water and help the crops grow better.

Student: ...water collection technology using "Ta-ta-ki." Do you all know *tataki*?

Narrator: After trial and error, they were able to triple the amount of water that could be stored. The fertilizer helped to **quadruple** the amount of corn harvested.

Miyaki: ❺ *Tataki* is a simple technique that involves mixing the necessary materials, (^{1}) (^{2}) (^{3}) (^{4}) (^{5}) (^{6}). ❻ We think that (^{1}) (^{2}) (^{3}) (^{4}) (^{5}) (^{6}) (^{7}) around the world.

❺ それから、土をたたいたり乾かしたりする

❻ それが環境問題を減らす助けとなる可能性がある

Narrator: ❼ To help farmers around the world learn about *tataki*, Miyaki and his team created an English manual and (^{1}) (^{2}) (^{3}) (^{4}) (^{5}) (^{6}). These efforts are helping their innovation, based on a traditional Japanese technique, to sprout worldwide.

❼ ただで入手できるようにした

各問、選択肢から適切な単語を選び、英文を完成させましょう。なお、余分な単語が1語ずつあります。

1. eスポーツと呼ばれるビデオゲームは、組織的で多人数で行う競技形式をとることがあります。

   A kind of (　　　　　) game competition, (＿＿＿＿＿) (＿＿＿＿＿)
   as e-sports, often (　　　　　) the (　　　　　) of (　　　　　),
   (　　　　　) competitions.

   > multiplayer　form　referred　video　to　triple　organized　takes

2. これからは、すべての新入社員にも同じ規則を適用します。

   We will (＿＿＿＿＿) the (　　　　　) (　　　　　) (＿＿＿＿＿) all the
   new (　　　　　) (　　　　　) now (　　　　　).

   > on　to　between　from　rule　apply　employees　same

3. 世界的な問題に、即時の解決法はない。ふつうは、試行錯誤の長い道のりとなる。

   There's no (　　　　　) way of (　　　　　) (　　　　　) to
   (　　　　　) problems. It is usually a long (　　　　　) of (＿＿＿＿＿)
   and (＿＿＿＿＿).

   > trial　quick　trivial　world　process　finding　error　solutions

4. この地域新聞は無料で作成・配布され、発行部数は3,000部です。

   This (　　　　　) newspaper is (　　　　　) and (　　　　　)
   (＿＿＿＿＿) of (＿＿＿＿＿) and (　　　　　) a (　　　　　) of 3,000.

   > charge　circulation　community　issue　distributed　has　produced　free

1. Are you interested in farming someday? If yes or maybe, what would you like to grow? If not, why not?

2. What season do you like best in Japan? Explain why.

UNIT 12

Green Tea Shochu Hits the Spot with Overseas Connoisseurs

新風味──お茶と焼酎のミックス

GREEN TEA SHOCHU HITS THE SPOT WITH OVERSEAS CONNOISSEURS

知覧といえば太平洋戦争の特攻隊を連想する人もいるが、飛行場があった広大な台地で農業が盛んな地域である。今、緑茶と芋焼酎の魅力を融合させた新たな味わいの焼酎が注目されている。緑茶は旨味豊かな一番茶葉を使い、さつまいもは南薩摩産を厳選している。それらが醸し出す新風味の芋焼酎が世界でも高い評価を得た。

放送日 2021/11/30

Words & Phrases

◎ CD 24

以下の単語や熟語の音声を聞きながら発音に注意し、意味を確認しましょう。

- [ ] to **hit the spot** 　　申し分ない、ちょうどいい
- [ ] **connoisseur** 　　鑑識者、玄人
- [ ] **beverage** 　　水以外の飲料
- [ ] **renowned** 　　有名な
- [ ] **sommelier** 　　ソムリエ
- [ ] **distilled** 　　蒸留した
- [ ] **dilution** 　　薄めること、希釈
- [ ] **fermented** 　　醗酵した
- [ ] **mash** 　　どろどろしたもの
- [ ] **thriving** 　　繁栄する
  - 例文 The small rural town developed into a *thriving* industrial city.
    その小さな田園の町は、繁栄する産業都市へと発展した。
- [ ] **aroma** 　　香り
  - 例文 The bakery was filled with the *aroma* of freshly baked bread.
    そのパン屋さんは、焼きたてのパンの香りであふれていた。

以下は、飲み物などに関する語彙です。1~10の空所に当てはまる英語を下のアルファベット表から見つけ、線で囲みましょう．囲み方は縦、横、斜めのいずれも可能です。

例　緑茶　　　　　　　　　　　（　　　**green**　　　）tea

● 炭酸飲料　　　　　　　　　　（　　　　　　　¹ ）drinks

● 麦茶　　　　　　　　　　　　（　　　　　　　² ）tea

● ほうじ茶　　　　　　　roasted tea

● ウーロン茶　　　　　　　　　（　　　　　　　³ ）tea

● 玄米茶　　　　　　　　　　　（　　　　　　　⁴ ）rice tea

● 豆乳　　　　　　　　　　　　（　　　　　　　⁵ ）milk

● アルコール飲料　　　　　　　（　　　　　　　⁶ ）beverages

● 生ビール　　　　　　　　　　（　　　　　　　⁷ ）beer

● ウィスキーの水割り　　　whisky and water

● シャンパン　　　　　　　　　（　　　　　　　⁸ ）

● 梅酒ロック　　　　　　　　　（　　　　　　　⁹ ）liquor on the rocks

● 水道水　　　　　　　　　　　（　　　　　　　¹⁰ ）water

	1	2	3	4	5	6	7	8	9	10	11	12	13	14	15	16
a	C	H	A	M	P	A	G	N	E	S	Q	A	N	B	C	S
b	G	P	A	P	A	L	C	O	H	O	L	I	C	A	A	O
c	R	E	G	G	P	O	U	U	D	B	V	X	S	R	L	Y
d	E	B	R	O	W	N	W	M	M	R	O	L	H	L	E	B
e	E	O	O	L	O	N	G	Z	L	O	A	S	T	E	D	E
f	N	Q	D	F	A	B	T	H	A	W	K	F	O	Y	Y	A
g	T	A	P	M	T	C	A	R	B	O	N	A	T	E	D	N

1st Viewing ≫ **Watch the News**

ニュースを見て、内容と合っているものはT、違っているものはFを選びましょう。

1. Imoshochu is mostly produced in the Kyushu district of Japan. 　T・F

2. Imoshochu won recognition in a worldwide sake master competition. 　T・F

3. Mori specializes in sweet potatoes but not green tea. 　T・F

1 ニュースをもう一度見て、各問の空所に入る適切な選択肢を a ~ c から選びましょう。

1. The sake master competition took place in _____.

   a. Kagoshima, Japan

   b. Paris, France

   c. London, England

2. Farmers make shochu in the fall and harvest tea leaves _____.

   a. only in spring

   b. during the same season

   c. in spring and summer

3. Demand for shochu has dropped, and demand for green tea has _____.

   a. remained the same

   b. increased

   c. also fallen

2 ニュースに関して、空所に入る適切な数字を枠内から選びましょう（余分な選択肢があります）。

1. (   ) brands participated in the distilled category of the sake master competition.

2. Mori's distillery began some (   ) years ago.

3. Production of shochu has decreased by (   ) % over the last (   ) years.

4. Mori's tea-flavored imoshochu costs (   ) % more than regular shochu.

| 10 | 13 | 30 | 50 | 80 | 100 | 130 | 146 | 164 | 184 |

Listen to the News Story

CDの音声を聞いて、News Story の ❶〜❼ の文中にある空所に適切な単語を書き入れましょう。音声は2回繰り返されます。

Anchor: Now, imoshochu is a type of alcohol made from sweet potatoes that is produced mostly in Japan's Kyushu region. ❶ A new **beverage** was recently launched that combines the strong flavor of the alcohol (¹) (²) (³) (⁴) (⁵) (⁶) (⁷) and is drawing attention overseas.

❶ 緑茶の洗練された
味つけの

Narrator: This is the Kura Master, a Japanese sake competition that was held in Paris in September. The judges are all **renowned** chefs and **sommeliers**. Of the 164 brands in the **distilled** sake category, the one that received the President's Award for most outstanding product is an imoshochu blended with green tea. ❷ The judges noted that the **dilution** with soda (¹) (²) (³) (⁴) (⁵) (⁶).

❷ お茶の繊細な風味
を引き立たせてい
る

The winning shochu comes from a small distillery in the town of Chiran in Kagoshima Prefecture, one of Japan's leading tea producing regions. A large amount of freshly picked green tea leaves from the first harvest of the season is added to the moromi, the **fermented mash** of sweet potatoes. ❸ Once distilled, the final result is a shochu (¹) (²) (³) (⁴) (⁵) (⁶) (⁷).

❸ 緑茶の独特な香り
のある

This is Mori Nobiru, the man behind the imoshochu. The Mori family has been cultivating green tea since about the same time the distillery was founded about 100 years ago. ❹ They make shochu in the fall and harvest tea leaves from spring to summer, which means they are (¹) (²) (³) (⁴) (⁵) (⁶).

❹ 1年の多くの時期
を通して忙しい

However, demand for both these products has fallen. Once

a **thriving** industry, shochu production in the region has declined by 30 percent over the past decade. As for green tea, sales of high quality leaves have dropped. ❺ So,

(¹) (²) (³)

(⁴) (⁵) (⁶),

Mori came up with the idea of combining imoshochu and green tea.

Mori Nobiru (President, Chiranjozo): It meant taking a step into the unknown, but after experimenting with these familiar ingredients, I found the final product very tasty.

Narrator: It was no easy task balancing the strong taste of shochu with the delicate flavor of green tea. It offered a chance for Mori, who until now has concentrated on both tastes separately, to put his skills to work. In order to settle on the final flavor, he tested ten varieties of tea, with imoshochu, to find the perfect combination. ❻ He finally decided (¹)

(²) (³) (⁴)

(⁵) (⁶) (⁷).

Mori: ❼ As a tea farmer, I strove to get a better **aroma**, and as a shochu maker, I (¹) (²)

(³) (⁴) (⁵)

(⁶) (⁷) of shochu.

Narrator: A singular product made by an expert of two local specialties, Mori's *tea-flavor*[*ed*] imoshochu may be 50 percent more expensive than regular shochu, but it is getting attention, and he plans to focus on expanding his sales overseas.

❺ 彼の商売を復活させよ
うと

❻ 自分が満足する割合に
ついて

❼ よい品質を引き出した
かった

Note: （p. 71）ℓ. 24　tea-flavor と発音されているが、文法的には tea-flavored
が正しい

各問、選択肢から適切な単語を選び、英文を完成させましょう。なお、余分な単語が1語ずつあります。

1. A: あなたのアップルパイは本当に美味しかった。
    B: 喜んでもらえてよかったです。

    A: Your apple pie (　　　　　　) (＿＿＿＿＿＿) (　　　　　　) (＿＿＿＿＿＿).
    B: Thanks. I'm (　　　　) (　　　　　　) (　　　　) it.

    | really | you | hit | the | enjoyed | good | glad | spot |

2. 彼はいい奴のようだ。でも仕事の能力のこととなるとそれは別の話だね。

    He (　　　　　) to be a (　　　　　　) (　　　　　). But (＿＿＿＿＿＿)
    (＿＿＿＿＿) his business ability, that's (　　　　　) (　　　　　).

    | another | seems | for | regarding | guy | as | matter | nice |

3. この経済状況で自分の生活のみではなく、将来のために備えるのは決して容易なことではない。

    It is (＿＿＿＿＿) (＿＿＿＿＿) task to (　　　　　) (　　　　　) in this
    (　　　　) and also (　　　　) money for the (　　　　　).

    | yourself | easy | economy | support | give | future | save | no |

4. 隣の部屋から絶えず騒音が聞こえて来たので、自分のやっていることに集中できなった。

    (　　　　　) of the (　　　　　) noise (　　　　　) (　　　　　) the
    next room, I couldn't (＿＿＿＿＿) (＿＿＿＿＿) (　　　　　) I was doing.

    | conclude | constant | on | because | coming | what | from | concentrate |

1. If you are over 20, what alcoholic or nonalcoholic beverages do you like best? If you are under 20, what are your favorite nonalcoholic drinks? Why?

2. What is the most memorable competition you were in? Did you win a prize? Explain.

UNIT 13

Looking to the Future in 'Jeans Town'

縫製ユーチューバー

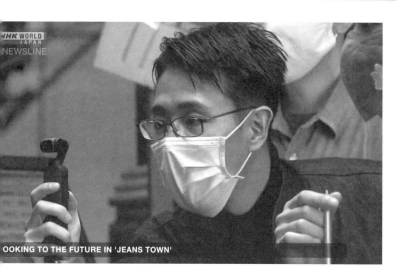

NHK WORLD JAPAN
NEWSLINE

LOOKING TO THE FUTURE IN 'JEANS TOWN'

アパレル業界で成功している起業家の話題である。福川太郎さんはGジャンに魅せられ、未経験からのスタートにもかかわらずデニムブランド「ダンジョデニム」を立ち上げた。また、仲間と共にYouTuberとして縫製バラエティーチャンネルに、デニム生地や縫製に関するユニークな動画を次々と投稿し人気を集めている。

放送日 2021/8/16

Words & Phrases

◉ CD 26

以下の単語や熟語の音声を聞きながら発音に注意し、意味を確認しましょう。

☐ **textile** 　織物、布地
☐ **steep** 　急激な
☐ to **carry on** 　〈商売〉を営む
☐ to **stand out** 　目立つ
☐ **distressed** 　古く見せた、着古した感じの
例文 Karen seems to love wearing *distressed* denim jeans.
　　カレンは、着古した感じのデニムジーンズが好きなようだ。
☐ to **come out** 　（結果として）出てくる、現れる
☐ **in-depth** 　詳細な
☐ **glossy** 　光沢のある、つやのある
☐ to **livestream** 　ライブ配信する
例文 My favorite YouTuber is *livestreaming* this evening.
　　私の好きなユーチューバーが、今晩ライブ配信する。
☐ **hat** 　《略式》肩書、地位、立場

Before You Watch

以下は、SNSに関するものです。下の枠内から適切な単語を選び、空所に入れましょう。

1. ツイッターのアカウント持っていますか。
   Do you have a (　　　　　　　) (　　　　　　　　　)?

2. フェイスブックを使っています。
   I'm (　　　　　　　) Facebook.

3. ご自由にフォローして下さい。
   (　　　　　　　) (　　　　　　　　　) to (　　　　　　) me.

4. 友だち追加ありがとうございます。
   Thank you for (　　　　　　　) me.

5. 「いいね！」をありがとう。
   Thank you for the (　　　　　　　).

6. あなたの投稿を見ました。
   I saw your (　　　　　　　).

7. 「いいね！」してね。
   Please give me a (　　　　　　　) up!

8. 日本語のSNSは、英語では「ソーシャルメディア」と言われています。
   Japanese "SNS" is (　　　　　　) (　　　　　　) (　　　　　　) in
   (　　　　　　).

9. "LOL" は、「大笑い」の略です。
   "LOL" is an abbreviation for "I'm (　　　　　　) (　　　　　　) loud."

10. "IMO" は、「私の考えでは」の略です。
    "IMO" is short for "in (　　　　　　) (　　　　　　)."

account	adding	called	English	feel	follow
free	laughing	like	media	my	on
opinion	out	post	social	thumbs	Twitter

1st Viewing ≫ Watch the News

ニュースを見て、内容と合っているものはT、違っているものはFを選びましょう。

1. Most Japanese textile companies have production factories in foreign countries.
   [T・F]

2. To introduce fabrics and sewing, Fukukawa posted a lot of TV style variety shows.
   [T・F]

3. One specific video shows distressed jeans produced using 300 firecrackers. [T・F]

1 ニュースをもう一度見て、各問の空所に入る適切な選択肢を a~c から選びましょう。

1. Lately textile artisans installed a YouTube channel showing videos on _____.

   a. how their fabrics are produced
   b. why Japanese fabrics are expensive
   c. how to correctly sew on zippers

2. Fukukawa is trying to realize his dream of _____.

   a. making lightweight hats from denim fabrics
   b. manufacturing his original denim jackets
   c. using Supima cotton to make better denim products

3. In one video, the artisan group showed how _____.

   a. much it cost to make a pair of denim jeans
   b. simple it is to promote denim products online
   c. long it took to produce a whole denim jacket

2 以下はニュースの概要です。空所に適切な単語を書き入れましょう。語頭の文字（群）は与えてあります。

Fukukawa Taro has long been interested in (**d** ¹) products. He moved to Okayama's Kojima district and started his career as a textile (**ar** ²). His goal is to manufacture his own original denim (**j** ³)《複数形》. Recently, he and other young artisans created a social media channel which introduces their (**fa** ⁴)《複数形》 and explains how they are made. Their videos look like those shown on TV (**v** ⁵) shows and are getting people interested in the textile industry.

CDの音声を聞いて、News Story の ❶〜❼ の文中にある空所に適切な単語を書き入れましょう。音声は2回繰り返されます。

Anchor: Japanese **textiles** have a worldwide reputation for excellence, but many companies have moved their production abroad to reduce labor costs. ❶ And this has led to a **steep** drop

     (¹) (²) (³)

❶ 若い人たちの数において

5   (⁴) (⁵) (⁶)

entering the industry in Japan. Now some textile artisans are working to enroll younger workers to **carry on** their business using social media platforms.

Narrator: ❷ The Kojima district of Okayama Prefecture is famous

10   as a center (¹) (²)

❷ ジーンズや他のデニム製品の製作のための

     (³) (⁴) (⁵)

     (⁶) (⁷). Recently, a group of young artisans set up a YouTube channel featuring videos about how they make their fabrics.

15   Fukukawa Taro moved to Kojima four years ago to pursue his dream to produce his own original denim jackets. The basic concept for the channel is to create a TV style variety show all about fabrics and machine sewing.

Fukukawa Taro (Danjo Denim): Most online videos about sewing are

20   practical guides such as how to sew on a zipper. ❸ We

❸ 私たちの動画が目立つように作りたかった

     (¹) (²) (³)

     (⁴) (⁵) (⁶)

     (⁷).

(A video countdown scene is shown. "Three, two, one, doozo.")

25 **Narrator:** This video shows the team trying to create **distressed** denim jeans using 3,000 firecrackers. This is how it **came out**.

Fukukawa: Ah, I see. Not so good.

Narrator: In another video, the team tried their hand at making a whole denim jacket to see how long it took.

30 **Man:** Two hours, six minutes, seven seconds.

Narrator: ❹ On this day, Fukukawa (¹)

(²) (³) (⁴)

(⁵) (⁶) to report on how
the fabrics are made. He asks **in-depth** questions to show
viewers the expertise that goes into the manufacturing
process. His focus this time is on the extra-fine Supima cotton
threads used by this producer.

Fukukawa: Supima cotton has long, smooth, **glossy** fibers.

❺ (¹) (²)

(³) (⁴) (⁵)

(⁶) (⁷), but we use three or
four threads together.

Narrator: ❻ Fukukawa is about to realize his dream of

(¹) (²) (³)

(⁴) (⁵) (⁶).

Fukukawa: That will be my workspace with my sewing machines.

Narrator: He plans to **livestream** on YouTube, so customers can watch
him at work on his sewing machines and also place orders.

Fukukawa: ❼ I hope some of our viewers will see that sewing
denim can be cool and more people (¹)

(²) (³) (⁴)

(⁵) (⁶).

Narrator: As a denim artisan and also as a YouTuber, Fukukawa will
continue to wear two **hats** as he pursues his dream.

❹ 地域の織物業者を訪れ
ている

❺ ほとんどのデニムが一
本の糸で作られている

❻ 彼自身の仕事場を作る

❼ 私たちの織物産業に興
味を持つようになる

各問、選択肢から適切な単語を選び、英文を完成させましょう。なお、余分な単語が1語ずつあります。

1. 学生たちの（ための）学園祭の組織委員会が立ち上げられた。

   A ( ) has ( ) (＿＿＿＿＿＿) (＿＿＿＿＿＿) to
   ( ) a campus ( ) for ( ).

festival	set	organize	committee	being	students	up	been

2. きょうの話し合いは、特に地球温暖化を和らげるのに私たちは何をすべきか、という環境問題の解決法に焦点を当て［特化し］ます。

   Today's discussion program (＿＿＿＿＿＿) solutions to ( )
   ( ), especially ( ) we ( ) do to reduce
   ( ) (＿＿＿＿＿).

global	features	what	problems	should	avoids	warming	environmental

3. 彼は自らベンチャー企業を立ち上げるという生涯の夢を追求することに決めた。

   He ( ) to (＿＿＿＿＿) ( ) ( )
   (＿＿＿＿＿) of ( ) his own venture business.

his	starting	dream	decided	refrain	lifelong	pursue

4. 彼女は肩書が二つある。大学の名誉教授と賞を獲得した小説家である。

   She (＿＿＿＿＿) (＿＿＿＿＿) (＿＿＿＿＿): an ( ) college
   professor and a ( ) ( ).

wears	novelist	emeritus	jackets	hats	prize-winning	two

1. Do you like denim jackets or jeans? Why or why not?

2. What kinds of clothes (styles, fabrics and colors) do you like? Explain.

A Recollection of Courage

UNIT 14

9.11 テロ、消防士の想い

Imura Keizo

SYMBOL OF RESPECT SENT TO NY FIREFIGHTERS

ニューヨーク市で同時多発テロが起きてから20年が経過した。これに対し長崎市消防局の元消防士、井村啓造さんら有志が、ニューヨーク市消防局に同事件で殉職した消防士を追悼する手ぬぐいや千羽鶴等を寄贈した。米側の担当者からは「皆さんの思いやりに深く感謝します。20年はあっという間でした」というメッセージが届いた。

放送日 2021/5/20

Words & Phrases

CD 28

以下の単語や熟語の音声を聞きながら発音に注意し、意味を確認しましょう。

- ☐ recollection 　　　思い出
- ☐ deadly 　　　致命的な、命取りの
- ☐ firefighter 　　　消防士、消防隊員
- ☐ to box up 　　　～を箱に詰める

　例文 Workers at the toy factory are *boxing up* dolls to sell at Christmas.
　　　そのおもちゃ工場の従業員たちは、クリスマスで販売する人形を箱詰めしている。

- ☐ to put one's life on the line 　《米語》命がけで行う
- ☐ to commemorate 　　～をたたえる
- ☐ tourniquet 　　　《医学》止血帯
- ☐ condolences 　　　〈複数形〉哀悼の言葉

　例文 He expressed his *condolences* to his uncle at the funeral.
　　　彼は葬式で伯父に対して弔意を表した。

- ☐ ultimate 　　　究極の、最大の
- ☐ in harm's way 　　　危険な状態に

Before You Watch

以下は、PC語 (politically correct、非差別的な) に関する表現です。下の枠内から適切な単語を選び、空所に入れましょう。

〈日本語〉	〈PC語〉		〈従来の表現〉
1. 消防士	fire ( )	←	fireman, firewoman
2. 警察官	police ( )	←	policeman, policewoman
3. 客室乗務員	flight ( )	←	steward, stewardess
4. アメリカ原住民	( ) American	←	American Indian
5. 黒人	( )-American	←	Black
6. 高齢者	( ) citizen	←	old person
7. 女性の俳優	( )	←	actress
8. ウエイター、ウエイトレス	( )	←	waiter, waitress
9. セールスマン	sales ( )	←	salesman, saleswoman
10. 障がい者	person with ( )	←	handicapped person
11. 視覚障がい者	a person with a visual ( )	←	blind

> actor　　African　　attendant　　disabilities　　fighter　　impairment
> Native　　officer　　representative　　senior　　server

1st Viewing ≫ Watch the News

ニュースを見て、内容と合っているものはT、違っているものはFを選びましょう。

1. During the terrorist attacks on New York, about 3,000 people were killed.　　T・F

2. Imura says he always thought that he would die on the job.　　T・F

3. Imura explains how *tenugui* can be used for various emergencies.　　T・F

1 ニュースをもう一度見て、各問の空所に入る適切な選択肢を a ~ c から選びましょう。

1. Imura worked as a firefighter for approximately
   _____.

   a. four years in New York
   b. 24 years in Nagasaki
   c. 40 years in Kyushu

2. Of the people who died in the terrorist attack on New
   York, _____.

   a. more than one in ten were firefighters
   b. over 1 % were Japanese
   c. several hundred of them were on-duty police
      officers

3. According to Imura, *tenugui* are _____.

   a. a symbol of peace
   b. carried for good luck
   c. commonly used in New York

2 右の文字列を並べ替えて単語を作り、各文の空所に入れて意味がとおるようにしましょう。

1. Many people were killed in the (   ) attack in New York 20 years ago.

   [rorirtest]

2. After working most of his life as a firefighter, Imura is now (   ).

   [tedreir]

3. Former Japanese firefighters sent Japanese *tenugui* hand (   ) to
   New York.
   [ewlots]

4. Two (   ) ago, Imura sent an American flag with messages.

   [deadecs]

Listen to the News Story

CDの音声を聞いて、News Story の ❶〜❼ の文中にある空所に適切な単語を書き入れましょう。音声は２回繰り返されます。

Anchor: This year marks 20 years since the **deadliest** terrorist attack to ever hit the United States. About 3,000 Americans were killed in the attack on New York's World Trade Center, including 24 Japanese and hundreds of **firefighters**.

5 ❶ As we see in this next report, (¹)

(²) (³) (⁴)

(⁵) (⁶) (⁷).

Narrator: Imura Keizo spent some four decades fighting fires in Nagasaki. Now retired, he and some of his colleagues

10 have been **boxing up** gifts to send to New York. ❷ They designed the presents themselves, (¹)

(²) (³) (⁴)

(⁵) (⁶) called *tenugui*.

Nearly 3,000 people died in the terrorist attacks on

15 September 11, 2001. Of those, 343 were on-duty firefighters. Imura was inspired by the New York firefighters' bravery, **putting** their lives **on the line** to save others.

Imura Keizo: I never went to a scene thinking this might be where I die. Those New York firefighters must have realized the danger

20 they faced on 9-11.

Narrator: Twenty years later, Imura and other retired coworkers decided to do something to **commemorate** the 343 firefighters who lost their lives. They sent the same number of *tenugui* towels to the New York City Fire Department.

25 ❸ Hand towels (¹) (²)

(³) (⁴) (⁵)

(⁶), but they have particular importance to firefighters in Japan.

Imura: When smoke builds up, we wet these towels and cover our

30 mouths with them. They also can function as **tourniquets**.

❹ (¹) (²) (³)

❶ ここの消防士は勇敢さを失くしていない

❷ 一種の、日本のハンドタオル

❸ 珍しいものを選んだように思われるかもしれない

❹ これらのようなタオルは様々な使い方がある

82

(4) (5) (6)
(7). We also carry them as symbols of good
luck.

Narrator: Two decades ago, Imura sent an American flag to the New
York Fire Department, inscribed with **condolences**.

(*The following message is shown on the screen.*)
As friends, we honor those in New York who made their
ultimate sacrifice and their colleagues.

❺ He treasures a T-shirt he received in return, a

❺ きずなと尊敬の象徴で
ある

(1) (2) (3)
(4) (5) (6)
for one another.

Over the past year, the pandemic has put public safety
personnel **in harm's way** again. Yet another reason to offer
moral support.

Imura: ❻ Our gift will let the firefighters in New York know we're

❻ 彼らのことを思い、健
康を願っている

(1) (2) (3)
(4) (5) (6)
(7).

Narrator: ❼ The hand towels may be simple, but (1)

❼ それらは有形の象徴を
提供する

(2) (3) (4)
(5) of holding on to hope.

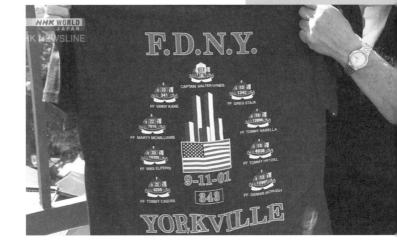

各問、選択肢から適切な単語を選び、英文を完成させましょう。なお、余分な単語が1語
ずつあります。

1. 人々は、国を守るのに命を懸ける軍人たちを名誉に思う。

   People (   ) the (   ) who (_____) (_____)
   (_____) on the (   ) defending their country.

lives	honor	line	soldiers	their	show	put

2. その作家の生誕200年を記念して銅像が建てられた。

   A (   ) (   ) (   ) to (_____) the 200th
   (   ) of the novelist's (   ).

erected	commemorate	statue	was	birth	memorize	anniversary

3. 建物を清掃したり芝生を刈ったりするのを手伝うと、テナントたちはそのお返しに［報酬として］
   家賃が減額になる。

   Tenants can (   ) rent (   ) in (_____) for
   (   ) to (   ) the building and (   ) the
   (   ).

helping	give	mow	get	lawn	return	clean	reductions

4. アメリカの警察官たちは時々危険にさらされる。

   (   ) (   ) in America (   ) often (   )
   in (_____) (   ).

officers	way	are	experienced	put	harm's	police

1. What news event or occurrence moved you recently? Explain.

2. Would you take a civil service job as a firefighter or police officer? Why or why not?

UNIT 15
Indoor Farms Sprouting Up in Cities

最新技術で都市型農業

DOOR FARMS SPROUTING UP IN CITIES

今、都市型の農法や販売の仕方が注目されている。スーパーの屋上で野菜を収穫し、下の店で販売するというものや、屋内で気温制御を使った水耕栽培で、薬草や野菜を収穫するというものである。いずれも生産地から販売店までの輸送コストや時間を撤廃でき、新鮮かつ栄養豊富な野菜を入手できるのが魅力である。

放送日 2021/5/12

Words & Phrases

 CD 30

以下の単語や熟語の音声を聞きながら発音に注意し、意味を確認しましょう。

☐ to **sprout up**　　次々出てくる

例文 New homes are *sprouting up* in areas that used to be farmland.
　　農地だった場所に今、次々と家が建てられてきている。

☐ **produce**　　　　農作物
☐ **populated**　　　密集した
☐ **snap pea**　　　　スナップエンドウ
☐ to **track**　　　　～を（追って）調べる
☐ **subsidiary**　　　子会社
☐ **cilantro**　　　　コリアンダー〈cf. coriander とも言う〉
☐ **hydroponic**　　　水耕栽培の、水栽培の
☐ **vertically**　　　縦に
☐ **emission**　　　　〈複数形〉排気
☐ **untapped**　　　　利用されていない、未開発の

例文 The project team is looking for new, *untapped* sources of energy.
　　そのプロジェクトチームは、新しい未開発のエネルギー源を探している。

以下は、野菜に関する単語です。空所に当てはまる英語を下のアルファベット表から見つけ、線で囲みましょう。囲み方は縦、横、斜めいずれも可能です。

例	だいこん	(**radish**)
1.	ピーマン	(**b**) pepper
2.	たけのこ	( ) shoot
3.	大豆	(**s**)
4.	もやし	( ) sprout
5.	とうがらし	(**c**) pepper
6.	ごぼう	(**b**)
7.	れんこん	(**l**) root
8.	しょうが	(**g**)
9.	ごま	( )
10.	ズッキーニ	( )
11.	パセリ	( )

	1	2	3	4	5	6	7	8	9	10	11	12	13	14	15	16
a	R	S	G	G	L	G	G	B	O	Z	Z	C	B	B	C	C
b	A	L	O	T	U	S	I	O	E	G	I	O	A	U	H	O
c	D	O	E	Y	P	O	N	N	P	A	P	O	M	M	I	I
d	I	W	E	B	B	A	G	I	G	O	N	P	B	E	L	L
e	S	E	S	A	M	E	A	C	E	E	L	E	O	O	I	I
f	H	P	A	S	S	I	A	E	B	U	R	D	O	C	K	L
g	B	Z	U	C	C	H	I	N	I	P	A	R	S	L	E	Y

ニュースを見て、内容と合っているものは T 、違っているものは F を選びましょう。

1. Most people living in urban areas buy vegetables cultivated in their cities. T・F

2. This rooftop garden in Shibuya is constantly monitored by an automatic system.

    T・F

3. In this supermarket's indoor farm, LEDs are used in place of sunlight. T・F

1 ニュースをもう一度見て、各問の空所に入る適切な選択肢を a ~ c から選びましょう。

1. This rooftop garden in Shibuya Ward is operated by _____.

    a. the local government

    b. a private company

    c. a group of land owners

2. In this supermarket's indoor farm, _____.

    a. the hydroponic method is being used

    b. planting and harvesting are managed by different companies

    c. carbon emissions are a serious problem

3. Indoor farms are being used _____.

    a. exclusively in Japan

    b. in 30 cities around the world

    c. by 10 Southeast Asian countries

2 以下は、紹介された2種類の農法に関した説明です。Rooftop にあてはまるものには（RT）、Indoor Farm に当てはまるものには（IF）の文字を空所に書き入れましょう。

1. Natural sunlight is used for growing vegetables.   (   )

2. This farming uses vertical space to grow plants.   (   )

3. People do not usually work on this kind of farm.   (   )

4. A sensor checks how moist the soil is.   (   )

5. Cultivation is done using the hydroponic method.   (   )

CDの音声を聞いて、News Story の ❶〜❼ の文中にある空所に適切な単語を書き入れましょう。音声は2回繰り返されます。

Anchor: Many consumers living in urban areas, such as Tokyo, buy most of their vegetables grown outside this city, but as our next story shows, an experimental form of agriculture is using the latest AI technologies to cultivate **produce** in **populated** areas.

Narrator: On the rooftop of this building in Shibuya Ward, Tokyo, about 20 kinds of *vegetable*[s], such as daikon radishes and **snap peas**, are being cultivated. It's run by a Tokyo start-up.

❶ The garden is usually left unattended, but the

(¹) (²) (³)
(⁴) (⁵) (⁶).

The device contains a sensor that monitors the light level and a camera that checks the growth of the vegetables. An additional sensor **tracks** the soil's moisture.

The data in the device is collected through the Internet and analyzed by AI. If the moisture level drops below 20 percent, the AI sends an alert to a smartphone that is registered through a membership system. ❷ The (¹)
(²) (³) (⁴)
(⁵) (⁶) (⁷).

The membership is free.

Serizawa Takayoshi (Co-founder & CEO, Plantio): Anyone can efficiently grow vegetables in a timely manner by digitalizing the process. ❸ I hope more people will (¹)
(²) (³) (⁴)
(⁵) (⁶) (⁷).

Narrator: Another emerging trend is to grow produce in supermarkets. In January, a Japanese **subsidiary** of a Germany start-up rented this supermarket space and built this facility. Italian basil and **cilantro** are cultivated here.

❶ (その) 野菜はこの装置を通して監視される

❷ (その) 装置は約〜ドルで販売される

❸ このような場所で農園を始める

Woman 1: ❹ I came as I heard there's (1)
(2) (3) (4)
(5) (6) (7).

Woman 2: Great smell.

5 **Narrator:** LED light has replaced sunlight, and the **hydroponic**
method enables the space to be utilized **vertically**. Staff
members manage the cultivation process from planting
to harvesting. The supermarket sells the vegetables for
about two dollars per bunch and divides the profits with the
10 company. The indoor farm has been launched in 30 cities
in 10 countries. ❺ The company hopes that it will reduce
carbon **emissions** by (1) (2)
(3) (4) (5)
(6).

15 *Hiraishi Ikuo (Managing Director, Infarm Japan):* People can grow vegetables in
their supermarkets and sell them there. ❻ I hope to
(1) (2) (3)
(4) (5) (6)
as much as I can.

20 **Narrator:** ❼ Even in a large city like Tokyo, there are still many empty
spaces and rooftops (1) (2)
(3) (4) (5)
(6) (7). The tremendous
potential for agriculture in the urban environment is still
25 **untapped**.

❹ スーパーにある一種の農地

❺ 作物を輸送する必要性を失くすことによって

❻ 農業のこの新しい考え方を促進する

❼ 野菜庭園に変えられる

Note: （p. 88）ℓ. 7　vegetable には -s が必要

各問、選択肢から適切な単語を選び、英文を完成させましょう。なお、余分な単語が１語
ずつあります。

1. このサービスを利用するには、旅券や車の免許証等この国での居住証明書を示す必要があります。

   To use this service, you have to show (　　　　　) of (　　　　　) in this
   (　　　　　), (＿＿＿＿＿) (　　　　　) a passport or a (　　　　　)
   (　　　　　) card.

insurance	country	as	so	residence	medical	such	proof

2. リサが別の課に異動になるので、誰か彼女に代わる人が必要だ。

   Lisa is (　　　　　) (　　　　　) to (　　　　　) (　　　　　), so we
   need (　　　　　) to (＿＿＿＿＿) (　　　　　).

her	being	department	transferred	someone	another	replace	gone

3. まだ若いうちに、できるだけ（多く）お金を稼ぎ、貯蓄したい。

   I want to (　　　　　) (　　　　　) and (　　　　　) as (＿＿＿＿＿)
   as I (＿＿＿＿＿) (　　　　　) I am (　　　　　) young.

many	still	make	money	while	save	can	much

4. 衣服が多すぎるよ。小さなベッドルームをウォークインクロゼットに変えたらどうだろう。

   We (　　　　　) so (　　　　　) (　　　　　) now. (　　　　　)
   (　　　　　) we (＿＿＿＿＿) our small bedroom (＿＿＿＿＿) a walk-in
   closet?

convert	why	many	have	lot	into	clothes	don't

1. Would you like to buy vegetables grown on rooftops or inside supermarkets? Why?
   What are the advantages or disadvantages? Explain.

2. What are your favorite vegetables? How do you prepare or cook them? Explain
   the steps.

このテキストのメインページ
www.kinsei-do.co.jp/plusmedia/41
次のページの QR コードを読み取る
直接ページにジャンプできます

オンライン映像配信サービス「plus⁺Media」について

本テキストの映像は plus⁺Media ページ（www.kinsei-do.co.jp/plusmedia）から、ストリーミング再生でご利用いただけます。手順は以下に従ってください。

ログイン

- ●ご利用には、ログインが必要です。
  サイトのログインページ（www.kinsei-do.co.jp/plusmedia/login）へ行き、plus⁺Media パスワード（次のページのシールをはがしたあとに印字されている数字とアルファベット）を入力します。

- ●パスワードは各テキストにつき1つです。
  有効期限は、<u>はじめてログインした時点から1年間</u>になります。

ログインページ

[利用方法]

次のページにある QR コード、もしくは plus⁺Media トップページ（www.kinsei-do.co.jp/plusmedia）から該当するテキストを選んで、そのテキストのメインページにジャンプしてください。

plus+Media トップ　　　メインページ

メニューページ　　　再生画面

「Video」「Audio」をタッチすると、それぞれのメニューページにジャンプしますので、そこから該当する項目を選べば、ストリーミングが開始されます。

[推奨環境]

iOS (iPhone, iPad)	OS: iOS 12 以降 ブラウザ：標準ブラウザ	Android	OS: Android 6 以降 ブラウザ：標準ブラウザ、Chrome
PC	OS: Windows 7/8/8.1/10, MacOS X　ブラウザ: Internet Explorer 10/11, Microsoft Edge, Firefox 48以降, Chrome 53以降, Safari		

※最新の推奨環境についてはウェブサイトをご確認ください。

※上記の推奨環境を満たしている場合でも、機種によってはご利用いただけない場合もあります。また、推奨環境は技術動向等により変更される場合があります。予めご了承ください。

このシールをはがすと
plus+Media 利用のための
パスワードが
記載されています。

一度はがすと元に戻すことは
できませんのでご注意下さい。

▲ここからはがして下さい

4170 NHK
NEWSLINE 6 plus+Media®

本書には音声 CD（別売）があります

NHK NEWSLINE 6
映像で学ぶ NHK 英語ニュースが伝える日本 6

2023年1月20日　初版第1刷発行
2023年2月20日　初版第2刷発行

編著者　　山﨑達朗
　　　　　Stella M. Yamazaki

発行者　　福岡正人

発行所　　株式会社　金星堂

（〒101-0051）東京都千代田区神田神保町 3-21
Tel. (03) 3263-3828（営業部）
(03) 3263-3997（編集部）
Fax (03) 3263-0716
https://www.kinsei-do.co.jp

編集担当　稲葉真美香　　　　　　　Printed in Japan
印刷所・製本所／大日本印刷株式会社

ISBN978-4-7647-4170-6 C1082